# Square up to GCSE Maths exams with CGP!

Psst. Want to do well in GCSE Maths? We'll tell you the secret to success — practise answering exam questions until you can do them in your sleep.

All right, so it's not much of a secret... but practice really is the only way to improve. That's why we've packed this brilliant CGP book with realistic exam-style questions, all beautifully matched to the latest Intermediate Level WJEC GCSE course!

We've also included detailed answers, so if you drop any marks, it's easy to find out exactly where you went wrong. When the real exams arrive, you'll be laughing.

# CGP — still the best! ☺

Our sole aim here at CGP is to produce the highest quality books — carefully written, immaculately presented and dangerously close to being funny.

Then we work our socks off to get them out to you — at the cheapest possible prices.

# Contents

✓ Use the tick boxes to check off the topics you've completed.

How to Use This Book.................................................................................................1
Exam Tips....................................................................................................................2

## Section One — Number

Calculations and Operations......................................................................................3
Negative Numbers......................................................................................................5
Rounding Numbers.....................................................................................................6
Estimating...................................................................................................................7
Bounds........................................................................................................................8
Special Types of Number...........................................................................................9
Multiples, Factors and Prime Factors......................................................................10
HCF and LCM..........................................................................................................12
Fractions...................................................................................................................13
Fractions, Decimals and Percentages.....................................................................15
Percentages..............................................................................................................17
Compound Growth and Decay................................................................................19
Ratios........................................................................................................................21
Direct and Inverse Proportion..................................................................................23
Powers and Roots....................................................................................................24
Standard Form.........................................................................................................25
Venn Diagrams.........................................................................................................27

## Section Two — Algebra

Simplifying Terms.....................................................................................................28
Expanding Brackets.................................................................................................29
Factorising................................................................................................................30
Expressions and Formulas.......................................................................................31
Solving Equations.....................................................................................................32
Formulas and Equations from Words......................................................................33
Rearranging Formulas.............................................................................................34
Quadratic Equations................................................................................................35
Trial and Improvement.............................................................................................36
Sequences................................................................................................................37
Inequalities...............................................................................................................39
Simultaneous Equations..........................................................................................41
Solving Equations Using Graphs.............................................................................42
Algebraic Proportion................................................................................................44
Coordinates and Midpoints......................................................................................45
Straight Lines...........................................................................................................46
Quadratic Graphs.....................................................................................................48
Real-Life Graphs......................................................................................................50
Travel Graphs...........................................................................................................51

## Section Three — Geometry and Measure

Symmetry ............................................................................................................ 53
Polygons ............................................................................................................. 54
Properties of 2D Shapes ..................................................................................... 55
Congruence and Similarity ................................................................................. 56
The Four Transformations .................................................................................. 57
More Transformation Stuff ................................................................................. 59
Perimeter and Area ............................................................................................. 60
Area — Circles .................................................................................................... 61
Nets and Surface Area ........................................................................................ 62
3D Shapes — Volume ......................................................................................... 63
Projections .......................................................................................................... 64
Conversions ........................................................................................................ 65
Compound Measures .......................................................................................... 67
Angles and Shapes .............................................................................................. 68
Parallel Lines ...................................................................................................... 70
Circle Geometry ................................................................................................. 71
Loci and Construction ........................................................................................ 73
Bearings and Scale Drawings .............................................................................. 75
Pythagoras' Theorem .......................................................................................... 77
Trigonometry — Sin, Cos, Tan ........................................................................... 78

## Section Four — Statistics

Planning an Investigation ................................................................................... 80
Sampling and Collecting Data ............................................................................ 81
Mean, Median, Mode and Range ....................................................................... 83
Averages and Spread .......................................................................................... 84
Simple Charts and Graphs .................................................................................. 85
Pie Charts ........................................................................................................... 86
Scatter Diagrams ................................................................................................ 87
Interpreting Data ................................................................................................ 88
Frequency Tables — Finding Averages ............................................................... 89
Grouped Frequency Tables ................................................................................. 90
Frequency Polygons and Diagrams ..................................................................... 91
Box-and-Whisker Plots ....................................................................................... 92
Cumulative Frequency ....................................................................................... 93
Probability Basics ............................................................................................... 95
Counting Outcomes ............................................................................................ 96
Relative Frequency ............................................................................................. 97
The And/Or Rules ............................................................................................... 99
Tree Diagrams .................................................................................................... 100
Probability from Venn Diagrams ........................................................................ 101

Answers .............................................................................................................. 102

Formula Sheet .................................................................................................... 124

Published by CGP

Editors:
Will Garrison, Shaun Harrogate, Tom Miles, Rosa Roberts, David Ryan, Ben Train, Ruth Wilbourne

With thanks to William Inge and Glenn Rogers for the proofreading.

ISBN: 978 1 78908 070 4

Clipart from Corel®
Printed by Elanders Ltd, Newcastle upon Tyne

Based on the classic CGP style created by Richard Parsons.

Text, design, layout and original illustrations © Coordination Group Publications Ltd. (CGP) 2018
All rights reserved.

Photocopying this book is not permitted, even if you have a CLA licence.
Extra copies are available from CGP with next day delivery • 0800 1712 712 • www.cgpbooks.co.uk

# How to Use This Book

- Hold the book upright, approximately 50 cm from your face, ensuring that the text looks like this, not sıɥʇ. Alternatively, place the book on a horizontal surface (e.g. a table or desk) and sit adjacent to the book, at a distance which doesn't make the text too small to read.
- In case of emergency, press the two halves of the book together firmly in order to close.
- Before attempting to use this book, familiarise yourself with the following safety information:

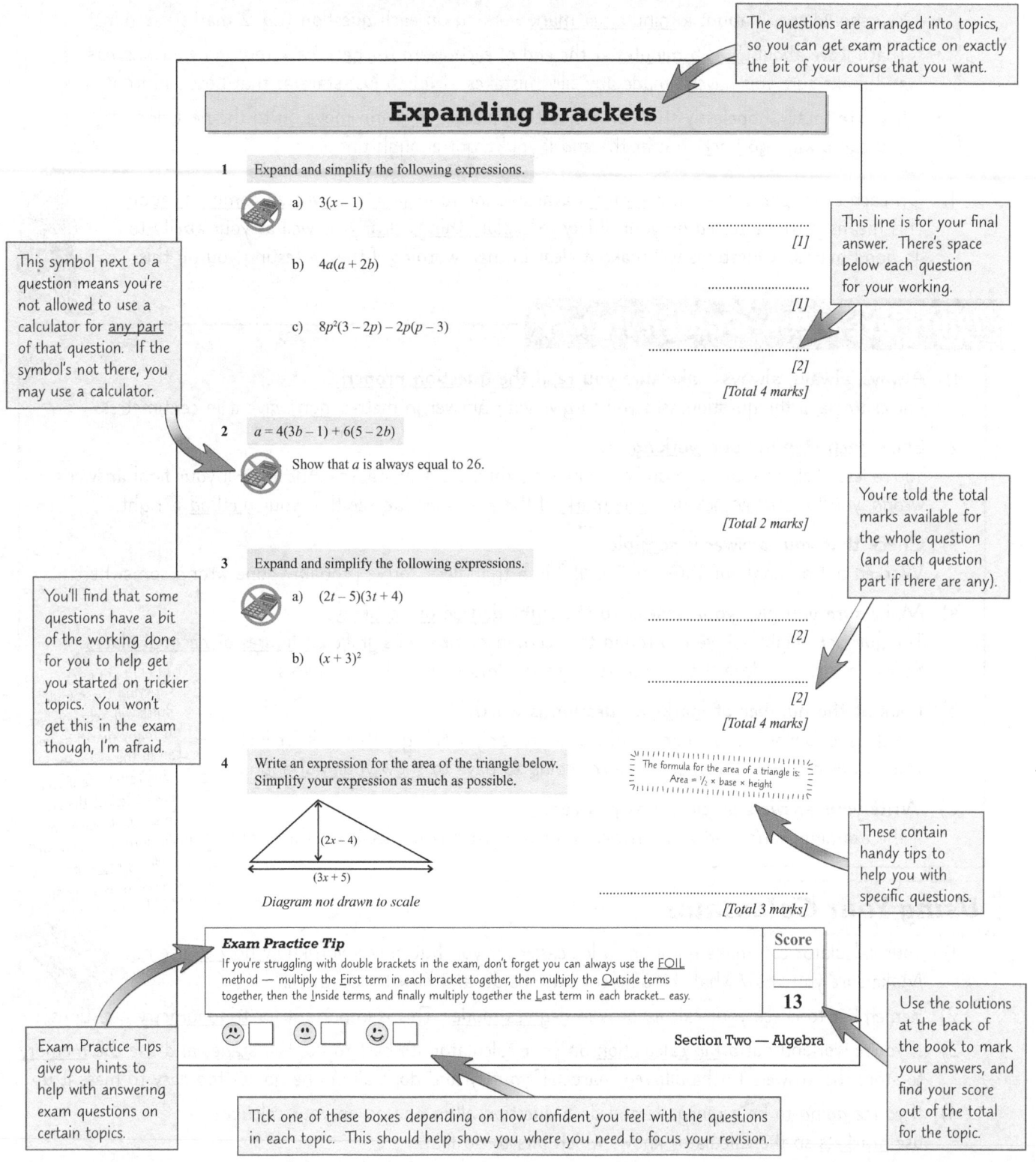

How To Use This Book

# Exam Tips

## Exam Stuff

1) You will have two exams — one non-calculator exam and one calculator exam.
2) Each exam is 1 hr 45 mins long and each is worth 80 marks.
3) Timings in the exam are really important, so here's a quick guide...

- You should spend about a minute per mark working on each question (e.g. 2 marks = 2 mins).
- That'll leave about 20-25 minutes at the end of each exam to check back through your answers and make sure you haven't made any silly mistakes. Not to just stare at that hottie in front.
- If you're totally, hopelessly stuck on a question, just leave it and move on to the next one. You can always go back to it at the end if you've got enough time.

4) On each exam paper, there are 2 marks available for your quality of written communication. This means you'll be tested on your ability to explain things clearly, as well as your ability to do good maths. Questions will make it clear in their wording if they're testing you on this.

## There are a Few Golden Rules

1) **Always, always, always make sure you read the question properly.**
   For example, if the question asks you to give your answer in metres, don't give it in centimetres.

2) **Show each step in your working.**
   You're less likely to make a mistake if you write things out in stages. And even if your final answer's wrong, you'll probably pick up some marks if the examiner can see that your method is right.

3) **Check that your answer is sensible.**
   Worked out an angle of 450° or 0.045° in a triangle? You've probably gone wrong somewhere...

4) **Make sure you give your answer to the right degree of accuracy.**
   The question might ask you to round to a certain number of significant figures or decimal places. So make sure you do just that, otherwise you'll almost certainly lose marks.

5) **Look at the number of marks a question is worth.**
   If a question's worth 2 or more marks, you probably won't get them all for just writing down the final answer — you're going to have to show your working.

6) **Write your answers as clearly as you can.**
   If the examiner can't read your answer you won't get any marks, even if it's right.

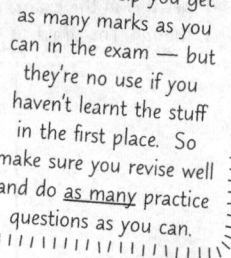

Obeying these Golden Rules will help you get as many marks as you can in the exam — but they're no use if you haven't learnt the stuff in the first place. So make sure you revise well and do as many practice questions as you can.

## Using Your Calculator

1) Your calculator can make questions a lot easier for you but only if you know how to use it. Make sure you know what the different buttons do and how to use them.

2) Remember to check your calculator is in degrees mode. This is important for trigonometry questions.

3) If you're working out a big calculation on your calculator, it's best to do it in stages and use the memory to store the answers to the different parts. If you try and do it all in one go, it's too easy to mess it up.

4) If you're going to be a renegade and do a question all in one go on your calculator, use brackets so the calculator knows which bits to do first.

REMEMBER: Golden Rule number 2 still applies, even if you're using a calculator — you should still write down all the steps you are doing so the examiner can see the method you're using.

# Section One — Number

## Calculations and Operations

**1** Work out 0.8 × 0.4.

.......... 0.32 ..........
[Total 1 mark]

**2** Calculate $\frac{4.2 \times 2.5}{9.1 - 5.9}$

Write down all the figures on your calculator display.

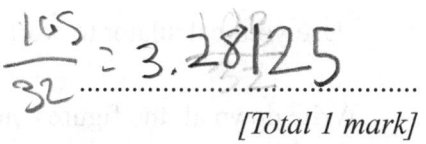

$\frac{105}{32}$ = 3.28125
[Total 1 mark]

**3** Work out:

a) 11 + 14 ÷ 2

14 ÷ 2 = 7
7 + 11 = 18

.......... 18 ..........
[2]

b) (20 − 15) × (4 + 6)

20 − 15 = 5
4 + 6 = 10
10 × 5 = 50

.......... 50 ..........
[2]
[Total 4 marks]

**4** Given that 56 × 427 = 23 912, find the value of:

a) 56 × 4270

.......... 23 9120 ..........
[1]

b) $\frac{23\,912}{42.7}$

.......... ..........
[1]

c) 5.6 × 4.27

.......... ..........
[1]
[Total 3 marks]

Section One — Number

5   Given that 34 × 48.2 = 1638.8, find the value of:

a)   3.4 × 4.82

.................
[1]

b)   340 × 0.482

.................
[1]

c)   $\dfrac{163.88}{482}$

.................
[1]

[Total 3 marks]

6   Use your calculator to work out $\dfrac{197.8}{\sqrt{0.01 + 0.23}}$.

Write down all the figures on your calculator display.

*This question is worth two marks so you'll need to show some working as well as the final answer.*

..............................
[Total 2 marks]

7   Use your calculator to work out $\sqrt{\dfrac{12.71 + 137.936}{\cos 50° \times 13.2^2}}$.

Write down all the figures on your calculator display.

..............................
[Total 2 marks]

**Exam Practice Tip**

The thing to keep in mind while doing calculations is that they are all about the order in which you do the operations. Always keep BODMAS in mind while you're working stuff out and you won't go too far wrong... So — Brackets, Other, Division, Multiplication, Addition, Subtraction. Got it? Perfect.

Score

16

Section One — Number

# Negative Numbers

**1** Work out:

a)  4 + –5

...........................
[1]

b)  –2 – –6

...........................
[1]

*[Total 2 marks]*

**2** Three numbers multiply to give 288. Two of the numbers are –3 and 12.

What is the third number?

...........................
*[Total 3 marks]*

**3** Put the numbers below in order from lowest to highest.

0.75     –0.23     –0.61     0.35     1.06     –1.12

............ , ............ , ............ , ............ , ............ , ............
*[Total 1 mark]*

**4** Priyanka has three number cards.

| –4 | 3 | 5 |

She is going to use the numbers to make a new number.
She can use the operations +, –, ×, ÷ and brackets.
What is the highest number she can make?

...........................
*[Total 3 marks]*

Score: 
9

Section One — Number

# Rounding Numbers

**1** Circle the answer that is 0.30284 rounded to:

a) 2 significant figures.

               0.3          0.32          0.302          0.30

*[1]*

b) 3 decimal places.

               0.30          0.302          0.303          0.31

*[1]*

*[Total 2 marks]*

**2** The distance between two stars is 428.6237 light years.

a) Round this distance to one decimal place.

.............................. light years
*[1]*

b) Round this distance to 2 significant figures.

.............................. light years
*[1]*

*[Total 2 marks]*

**3** Use your calculator to find:

$$\frac{4.32^2 - \sqrt{13.4}}{16.3 + 2.19}$$

Give your answer to 3 significant figures.

..............................
*[Total 2 marks]*

**4** A number rounded to the nearest whole number is 122.

What is the smallest possible value of the number?

..............................
*[Total 1 mark]*

Score:

Section One — Number

# Estimating

1   The man in this picture is 180 cm tall.

Use this information to estimate the height of the penguin.

.................... cm
*[Total 2 marks]*

2   Estimate the value of $\dfrac{12.2 \times 1.86}{0.19}$

*You should start by rounding each number to an easier one.*

..........................
*[Total 2 marks]*

3   Look at the following calculation: $\dfrac{215.7 \times 44.8}{460}$

 a) By rounding each number to 1 significant figure, give an estimate for $\dfrac{215.7 \times 44.8}{460}$.

..........................
*[2]*

b) Will your answer to part a) be larger or smaller than the exact answer? Explain why.

...................................................................................................................................

...................................................................................................................................
*[2]*
*[Total 4 marks]*

4   Work out an estimate for $\sqrt{\dfrac{2321}{19.673 \times 3.81}}$

 Show all of your working.

..........................
*[Total 3 marks]*

Score: ☐
11

Section One — Number

# Bounds

**1** Morgan weighs 57 kg to the nearest kilogram.

What are the minimum and maximum weights that he could be?

Minimum weight: .................... kg

Maximum weight: .................... kg

*[Total 2 marks]*

**2** The width of a rectangular piece of paper is 23.6 centimetres, correct to 1 decimal place. The length of the paper is 54.1 centimetres, correct to 1 decimal place.

a) Write down the lower bound for the length of the paper.

.................... cm
*[1]*

b) Calculate the lower bound for the perimeter of the piece of paper.

.................... cm
*[2]*

*[Total 3 marks]*

**3** Given that $x = 2.2$ correct to 1 decimal place, find the interval that contains the value of $4x + 3$. Give your answer as an inequality.

........................................

*[Total 4 marks]*

**4** Bucket A has a volume of 8.3 litres and bucket B has a volume of 13.7 litres. Both measurements are to the nearest 0.1 litres.

Calculate the lower bound of the difference, in litres, between the volumes of bucket A and bucket B.

.................... litres
*[Total 2 marks]*

### Exam Practice Tip
Finding minimum and maximum values can be a bit tricky, as the amount you have to add and subtract changes depending on how the number's been rounded. Remember, you always add and subtract half of the rounding unit (so if you were rounding to the nearest 10, the number you'd add/subtract is 10 ÷ 2 = 5).

**Score** 11

# Special Types of Number

**1** Choose a number from the list which matches each description.

12   100   32   41   27   15   50

a) A square number.

........................
*[1]*

b) A cube number.

........................
*[1]*

*[Total 2 marks]*

**2** Write down the value of each of the following:

a) $4^3 + 6^2$

........................
*[2]*

b) $5^2 \times 3^2$

........................
*[2]*

c) $\sqrt{81} - 2^2$

........................
*[2]*

*[Total 6 marks]*

**3** "Adding two consecutive integers always gives an odd number."

Is the above statement true or false?  Circle the correct answer     TRUE     FALSE

Explain your answer.

..........................................................................................................................

..........................................................................................................................

*[Total 2 marks]*

Score:

Section One — Number

# Multiples, Factors and Prime Factors

**1** Rhys thinks of a prime number. The sum of its digits is one more than a square number.

Write down one number Rhys could be thinking of.

.........................
*[Total 2 marks]*

**2** Write down:

a) **all** the factors of 28,

.........................................
*[2]*

b) all the multiples of 8 which appear in the list below.

55  56  57  58  59  60  61  62  63  64  65

.........................................
*[1]*
*[Total 3 marks]*

**3** Write down two common factors of 24 and 36.

.................  .................
*[Total 2 marks]*

**4** Express:

a) 210 as a product of its prime factors.

.........................................
*[2]*

b) $105^2$ as a product of its prime factors in index form.

.........................................
*[2]*
*[Total 4 marks]*

Section One — Number

5   If *a* and *b* are prime numbers, give an example to show that each of the following statements is false:

a)  *a* + *b* is always even.

....................
[1]

b)  *a* × *b* is always odd.

....................
[1]

c)  $a^2 + b^2$ is always even.

*Remember — 1 is not a prime number.*

....................
[1]

[Total 3 marks]

6   Erica says "even square numbers always have more factors than odd square numbers". Find examples to show that Erica is wrong.

....................
[Total 2 marks]

7   A number, *x*, is a common multiple of 6 and 7, and a common factor of 252 and 420. Given that 50 < *x* < 150, find the value of *x*.

*x* = ............
[Total 4 marks]

**Exam Practice Tip**
Multiples, factors and prime factors can be a bit confusing at first. Remember, multiples of a number are the numbers that are in its times table, and factors are the numbers that divide into the original number. A prime factor is — yep, you guessed it — a factor that is also a prime number.

Score

20

Section One — Number

# HCF and LCM

1  $P = 3^7 \times 11^2$ and $Q = 3^4 \times 7^3 \times 11$.

Write as the product of prime factors:

a) the least common multiple (LCM) of $P$ and $Q$,

..................................
[1]

b) the highest common factor (HCF) of $P$ and $Q$.

..................................
[1]

[Total 2 marks]

2  $X = 2^8$, $Y = 2^5 \times 5^3$ and $Z = 2^6 \times 5^2 \times 7$.

Write as the product of prime factors:

a) the least common multiple (LCM) of $X$, $Y$ and $Z$,

..................................
[2]

b) the highest common factor (HCF) of $X$, $Y$ and $Z$.

..................................
[2]

[Total 4 marks]

3  $A$ and $B$ are different prime numbers. Find the least common multiple (LCM) of $A$ and $B$.

..................................
[Total 2 marks]

Score:

8

Section One — Number

# Fractions

**1** Find:

a) $\frac{3}{5}$ of 60,

..............................
*[2]*

b) 15 out of 40 as a fraction in its simplest form.

..............................
*[2]*

*[Total 4 marks]*

**2** Work out the following:

a) $\frac{1}{2} \times \frac{1}{6}$     $\frac{1}{2} \times \frac{1}{6} = \frac{\ldots \times \ldots}{\ldots \times \ldots} = \frac{\ldots}{\ldots}$

..............................
*[1]*

b) $\frac{2}{3} \div \frac{3}{5}$     $\frac{2}{3} \div \frac{3}{5} = \frac{2}{3} \times \frac{\ldots}{\ldots} = \frac{\ldots \times \ldots}{\ldots \times \ldots} = \frac{\ldots}{\ldots}$

..............................
*[2]*

*[Total 3 marks]*

**3** Which of these fractions is closest to 1?

$\frac{5}{6}$     $\frac{3}{4}$     $\frac{7}{8}$

..............................
*[Total 1 mark]*

**4** How many thirds are there in 12?

..............................
*[Total 1 mark]*

Section One — Number

**5** *ABC* is an equilateral triangle. It has been divided into smaller equilateral triangles as shown below.

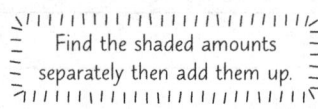

What fraction of triangle *ABC* is shaded?

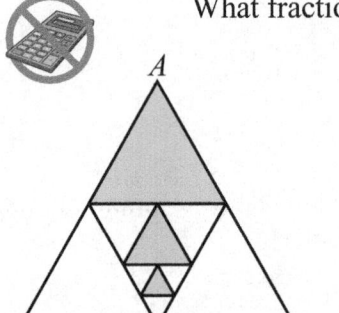

..........................
[Total 3 marks]

**6** Show that:

a) $\dfrac{4}{12} + \dfrac{3}{5} = \dfrac{14}{15}$

[2]

b) $\dfrac{9}{10} - \dfrac{2}{8} = \dfrac{13}{20}$

[2]
[Total 4 marks]

**7** Work out:

 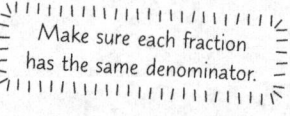

a) $3\dfrac{1}{2} + 2\dfrac{3}{5}$

..........................
[3]

b) $3\dfrac{3}{4} - 2\dfrac{1}{3}$

..........................
[3]
[Total 6 marks]

### Exam Practice Tip

Fractions — you can never get away from them, can you? Most of these questions require you to do it all by hand without a calculator. Don't rush when you're working stuff out and you'll be less likely to make silly mistakes. And always double-check which operation the question wants you to do.

Score: 22

# Fractions, Decimals and Percentages

**1** Convert each of the following:

  a) $\frac{3}{5}$ to a decimal.

  .................
  *[1]*

  b) 0.04 to a percentage.

  .................
  *[1]*

  c) 65% to a fraction in its simplest form.

  .................
  *[1]*

  *[Total 3 marks]*

**2** Write the following in order of size, starting with the smallest.

  65%     $\frac{2}{3}$     0.065     $\frac{33}{50}$

  *Start by writing all the numbers as decimals.*

  ...................... , ...................... , ...................... , ......................
  *[Total 3 marks]*

**3** There are 150 coloured blocks in a box. Each block is red, blue or green.

  42% of the blocks are red.

  $\frac{8}{25}$ of the blocks are blue.

  How many of the blocks are green?

  ......................
  *[Total 3 marks]*

Section One — Number

4    Write $\frac{10}{11}$ as a recurring decimal.

..............................
[Total 1 mark]

5    Find the reciprocal of 0.3 correct to 1 decimal place.

..............................
[Total 1 mark]

6    What fraction is equal to 25% of $\frac{1}{5}$?

..............................
[Total 1 mark]

7    A bill is split between four people.
     One person pays $\frac{1}{4}$ of the bill, two people each pay 20% and the other person pays £17.50.

     How much was the bill in total?

£ ..............................
[Total 4 marks]

**Exam Practice Tip**
Reciprocals and recurring decimals can sound pretty scary, but once you get to know them you'll see they aren't so bad, really. A good thing to remember is these two facts — the reciprocal of a number is always 1 divided by that number, and if you multiply a number by its reciprocal you get 1.

Section One — Number

# Percentages

**1** Work out 115% of 5200.

..........................
*[Total 2 marks]*

**2** What is 18 as a percentage of 60?

..........................
*[Total 1 mark]*

**3** A savings account offers 7% simple interest each year.
If £150 is invested, find the total amount of interest paid over 3 years.

..........................
*[Total 2 marks]*

**4** A computer costs £927 plus VAT, where VAT is charged at 20%.
Find the total cost of the computer.

£ ..........................
*[Total 2 marks]*

Section One — Number

**5** After an 8% pay rise a salary is £15 714.

What was the salary before the increase?

£ ..........................
[Total 2 marks]

**6** *x* is increased by 17% to 13 104.

What was the value of *x* before the increase?

..........................
[Total 2 marks]

**7** A TV is reduced by 20% for a sale event. After the event, the TV goes back to its original price.

What is the percentage increase in the TV's price at the end of the sale event?

..........................
[Total 3 marks]

**8** Bag *A* contains *a* balls and bag *B* contains *b* balls. 15% of the balls from bag *A* are removed and added to bag *B*. Both bags now contain an equal number of balls.

Express *b* as a percentage of *a*.

..........................
[Total 4 marks]

Section One — Number

# Compound Growth and Decay

1   Compound interest of 6% per annum is charged on a loan of £750.

*Per annum just means per year.*

What will the total amount owed be after 3 years of interest?
Give your answer to the nearest penny.

Multiplier = 1 + .................... = ....................

After 3 years the amount will be: .................... × (....................)⁻ = ....................

£ ..............................
*[Total 3 marks]*

2   The balance of a savings account, £B, is given by the formula $B = 5000 \times 1.02^t$ where $t$ is the number of years since the account was opened.

a)   What was the balance of the account when it was first opened?

£ ..............................
*[1]*

b)   How much is in the account after 7 years? Give your answer to the nearest penny.

£ ..............................
*[2]*

*[Total 3 marks]*

3   A car is travelling at 30 km/h. It starts to accelerate.
For every km it travels, its speed increases by 10%.

What will the car's speed be after it has travelled 5 km?
Give your answer to 3 significant figures.

................. km/h
*[Total 3 marks]*

Section One — Number

**4** The annual rate of depreciation of an object is 25%. If the object has an initial value of £10 000, what is its value after 5 years, to the nearest pound?

£ ...........................................

*[Total 2 marks]*

**5** A bank has two savings accounts.

| *Compound Interest Account* |
| --- |
| 5.5% compound interest per year, paid annually into your account. Rate is guaranteed for 5 years. |

| *Simple Interest Account* |
| --- |
| 6.2% simple interest paid annually by cheque. Rate guaranteed for 5 years, no further deposits permitted after opening. |

a) A customer has £10 000 to invest. Which one of the accounts should they put their money in to get the largest returns on the investment after 5 years?

................................................................

*[4]*

b) Why might the customer decide to put their money in the Compound Interest Account?

................................................................

................................................................

*[1]*

*[Total 5 marks]*

**6** A conservation company plants pine trees in a forest to increase their number by 16% each year. At the end of each year, a logging company is permitted to cut down up to 75% of the number of new trees planted that year.

At the start of 2016 there were 5000 pine trees in the forest.
What was the minimum number of pine trees in the forest at the end of 2017?

................................................................

*[Total 4 marks]*

Score:

20

Section One — Number

# Ratios

**1** Give the ratio 16 : 240 in its simplest form.

.........................
*[Total 2 marks]*

**2** A fruit punch is made of apple juice, pineapple juice and cherryade in the ratio 4 : 3 : 7.

a) What fraction of the fruit punch is pineapple juice?

.........................
*[1]*

b) There is 700 ml of fruit punch. What volume of each type of drink is used?

Apple juice: ........................ ml

Pineapple juice: ........................ ml

Cherryade: ........................ ml
*[3]*

*[Total 4 marks]*

**3** 84 is divided in the ratio 3 : 5 : 4 : 8.

What is the value of the largest share?

.........................
*[Total 2 marks]*

Section One — Number

4   Rhonda, Ariana, Nasir and Catrin shared £660.
Nasir got four times as much money as Catrin, Rhonda got twice as much money as Nasir, and Ariana got a quarter as much money as Rhonda.

How much money did Rhonda get?

£ ........................
[Total 3 marks]

5   A block of wood is divided in the ratio 3 : 6 : 7.
The largest piece weighs 300 g more than the smallest.

What was the weight of the original block of wood?

........................ g
[Total 4 marks]

6   A floor is made from red, green and white tiles. The ratio of red to green tiles in the floor is 1 : 3. The ratio of green to white tiles in the floor is 4 : 3.

Work out the fraction of tiles in the floor that are white.

Start by scaling up each ratio so the green amounts are equal.

........................
[Total 3 marks]

Score: 18

Section One — Number

# Direct and Inverse Proportion

**1** It takes 5 m² of cotton to make 8 T-shirts.
Cotton is sold per square metre. 2 m² of cotton costs £5.50.

How much will it cost to buy enough cotton to make 85 T-shirts?

£ ..........................
*[Total 4 marks]*

**2** Neil and Sian are harvesting some crops. Sian needs to harvest three times as many crops as Neil but she can harvest them twice as quickly.

Neil takes 3.5 hours to harvest his crops. How long does Sian take to harvest her crops?

.......................... hours
*[Total 3 marks]*

**3** It takes 12 litres of petrol to race 8 go-karts for 20 minutes. Petrol costs £1.37 per litre.

a) 6 go-karts used 18 litres of petrol. How many minutes did they race for?

.......................... minutes
*[4]*

b) How much does the petrol cost to run 8 go-karts for 45 minutes?

£ ..........................
*[3]*

*[Total 7 marks]*

**Exam Practice Tip**
Don't forget the golden rule for direct proportion — divide for one, then times for all. Sometimes you'll need to do this a few more times to find the answer, depending on what the question is asking. Tackle questions like this step by step and you'll be fine. And your joy will be in direct proportion to your understanding.

Score: 14

Section One — Number

# Powers and Roots

**1** Use your calculator to find the following:

a) $8.7^3$

.........................
[1]

b) $\sqrt[3]{729}$

.........................
[1]

c) $4^{-2}$

.........................
[1]

*[Total 3 marks]*

**2** Simplify the expression $\dfrac{3^4 \times 3^7}{3^6}$. Leave your answer in index form.

.........................
*[Total 2 marks]*

**3** Circle the value of each of the following:

a) $3^0$

        3       1       $\dfrac{1}{3}$       0       $-1$

[1]

b) $8^{\frac{1}{3}}$

      $\dfrac{1}{24}$       2       $-512$       $\dfrac{1}{512}$       $-2$

[1]

*[Total 2 marks]*

**4** Work out the value of:

$(2^4 \times 2^7) \div (2^3 \times 2^2)^2$

$(2^4 \times 2^7) = 2^{(\text{---} + \text{---})} = 2^{\text{---}}$

$(2^3 \times 2^2) = 2^{(\text{---} + \text{---})} = 2^{\text{---}}$, so $(2^3 \times 2^2)^2 = (2^{\text{---}})^2 = 2^{\text{---}}$

So $(2^4 \times 2^7) \div (2^3 \times 2^2)^2 = 2^{\text{---}} \div 2^{\text{---}} = 2^{\text{---}} = $ .........

.........................
*[Total 2 marks]*

Score:  9

# Standard Form

**1**    $A = 4.834 \times 10^9$, $B = 2.7 \times 10^5$, $C = 5800$

     a)    Express $A$ as an ordinary number.

..................................

*[1]*

     b)    Work out $B \times C$. Give your answer in standard form.

..................................

*[2]*

     c)    Put $A$, $B$ and $C$ in order from smallest to largest.

.........., .........., ..........

*[1]*

*[Total 4 marks]*

**2**    Express the following numbers in standard form:

     a)    648 200 000

..................................

*[1]*

     b)    0.0000245

..................................

*[1]*

*[Total 2 marks]*

**3**    What is $\dfrac{9.3 \times 10^7}{1.86 \times 10^5}$? Give your answer in standard form.

..................................

*[Total 2 marks]*

**4**    $A = (5 \times 10^5) + (5 \times 10^3) + (5 \times 10^2) + (5 \times 10^{-2})$

     Find the value of $A$. Give your answer as an ordinary number.

..................................

*[Total 2 marks]*

Section One — Number

**5** $A = 1.5 \times 10^8$ and $B = 4.5 \times 10^9$.

Write the ratio $A : B$ in the form $1 : n$.

..................................
[Total 3 marks]

**6** Work out:

a) $\dfrac{4 \times 10^{-4}}{8 \times 10^{-5}}$

Give your answer as an ordinary number.

..................................
[2]

b) $4 \times 10^{-4} + 6 \times 10^{-5}$
Give your answer in standard form.

TIP: you need matching powers to be able to add two numbers together in standard form.

..................................
[2]
[Total 4 marks]

**7** $A = 7.59 \times 10^7$, $B = 2.1 \times 10^5$ and $C = A + B$.

Find $C$, giving your answer in standard form.

..................................
[Total 2 marks]

Score:

19

Section One — Number

# Venn Diagrams

1   The universal set (ξ) = {1, 2, 3, 4, 5, 6, 7, 8, 9, 10, 11, 12}

   Set X = {x : x is an even number}.     Set Y = {y : y is a multiple of 3}.

   a) Use the information above to complete the Venn diagram.

   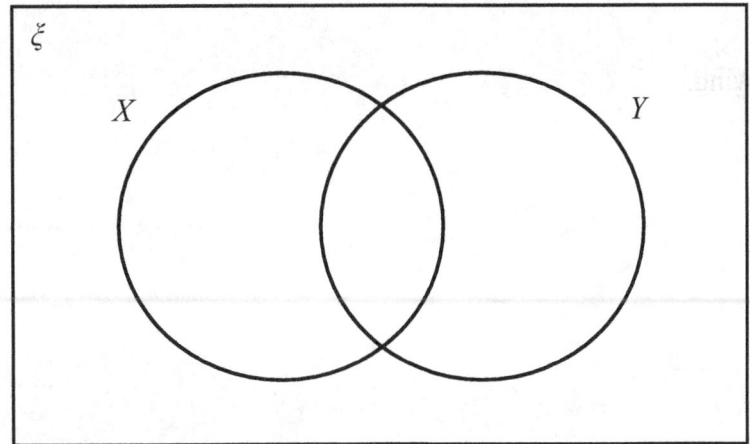

   [4]

   b) How many elements are in X'∩ Y?

   ...........................

   [1]

   c) How many elements are in X'∩ Y'?

   ...........................

   [1]

   [Total 6 marks]

2   A cheese stall sells Cheddar, Wensleydale and Stilton. Sales are recorded over one week.

   48 customers bought Cheddar. 28 customers bought Wensleydale. 52 customers bought Stilton.
   10 customers bought both Cheddar and Wensleydale.
   7 customers bought both Cheddar and Stilton.
   No customers bought both Wensleydale and Stilton.

   a) Use the information above to complete the Venn diagram.

   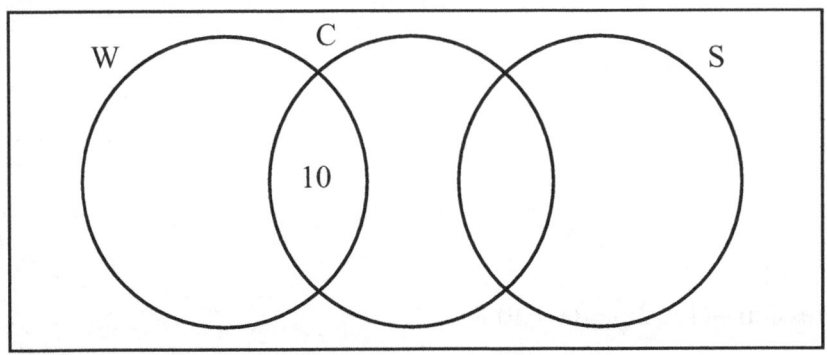

   [2]

   b) How many customers did the store have over one week?

   ...........................

   [1]

   [Total 3 marks]

   Score:

   9

# Simplifying Terms

**1** Circle the simplified version of $4s - 3s + 9s$.

$16s$ $\qquad$ $12s$ $\qquad$ $10s$ $\qquad$ $-8s$ $\qquad$ $11s$

*[Total 1 mark]*

**2** Simplify the following.

a) $p + p + p + p$

.........................
*[1]*

b) $m + 3m - 2m$

.........................
*[1]*

c) $7r - 2p - 4r + 6p$

.........................
*[2]*
*[Total 4 marks]*

**3** Write the following in their simplest form.

a) $2a \times 5b$

.........................
*[1]*

b) $5pq + pq - 2pq$

.........................
*[1]*

c) $2x^2 + 8x - 4x - x^2$

.........................
*[2]*
*[Total 4 marks]*

**4** Simplify the expression $-(1 + 2x) + (x + 9)$.

.........................
*[Total 2 marks]*

Score: 11

# Expanding Brackets

1   Expand and simplify the following expressions.

    a)   $3(x - 1)$

.................................
[1]

    b)   $4a(a + 2b)$

.................................
[1]

    c)   $8p^2(3 - 2p) - 2p(p - 3)$

.................................
[2]

*[Total 4 marks]*

2   $a = 4(3b - 1) + 6(5 - 2b)$

   Show that $a$ is always equal to 26.

*[Total 2 marks]*

3   Expand and simplify the following expressions.

    a)   $(2t - 5)(3t + 4)$

.................................
[2]

    b)   $(x + 3)^2$

.................................
[2]

*[Total 4 marks]*

4   Write an expression for the area of the triangle below.
Simplify your expression as much as possible.

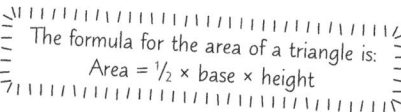

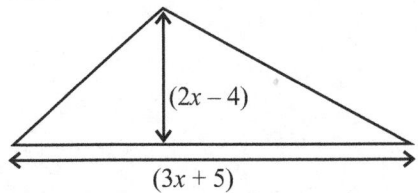

*Diagram not drawn to scale*

.................................
*[Total 3 marks]*

**Exam Practice Tip**

If you're struggling with double brackets in the exam, don't forget you can always use the FOIL method — multiply the First term in each bracket together, then multiply the Outside terms together, then the Inside terms, and finally multiply together the Last term in each bracket... easy.

Score

13

# Factorising

**1** Factorise the following expressions.

a) $6x + 3$

..........................................
[1]

b) $x^2 + 7x$

..........................................
[1]

c) $25p - 15q$

..........................................
[1]

[Total 3 marks]

**2** Factorise fully $8a^2 - 48ab$.

$8a^2 - 48ab = 8(\ldots\ldots - \ldots\ldots)$

$= 8 \ldots(\ldots\ldots - \ldots\ldots)$

..........................................
[Total 2 marks]

**3** Factorise the following expressions fully.

a) $16x + 4x^2$

..........................................
[2]

b) $25y^2 - 40y^3$

..........................................
[2]

c) $6v^2w^3 + 30v^4w^2$

..........................................
[2]

[Total 6 marks]

Score: ☐

**11**

# Expressions and Formulas

**1**  $S = 4m^2 + 2.5n$

a) Calculate the value of $S$ when $m = 2$ and $n = 10$.

S = (4 × .............. × ..............) + (2.5 × ..............)

S = .............. + ..............

S = ..............

.................................................
[2]

b) Calculate the value of $n$ when $S = 179$ and $m = 6.5$.

.................................................
[2]

[Total 4 marks]

**2**  Select the correct words from the box to complete the statements below.

| a formula | an equation | an expression | a function |

a) $4q - 5$ is .............................................. [1]

b) $x^2 + 3x = 0$ is .............................................. [1]

[Total 2 marks]

**3**  The function machine below shows the function 'add 7 and divide by 5'.

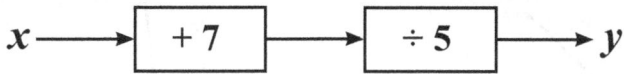

a) Find the value of $y$ when $x = 23$.

$y = $ ..............................
[1]

b) Find the value of $x$ when $y = 3$.

$x = $ ..............................
[2]

[Total 3 marks]

Score: 9

# Solving Equations

**1** Solve the following equations.

  a)  $7b - 5 = 3(b + 1)$

b = ..................
[3]

b)  $\dfrac{45 - z}{5} = 6$

z = ..................
[2]

[Total 5 marks]

**2** Solve this equation.

  $\dfrac{5 - 3x}{2} + \dfrac{6x + 1}{5} = 15$

x = ..................
[Total 4 marks]

**3** The quadrilateral below has a perimeter of 67 cm.

 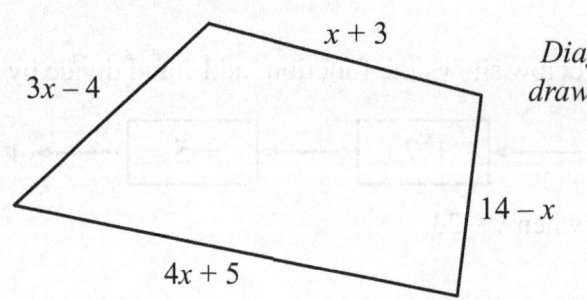

*Diagram not drawn to scale*

All of the lengths on this diagram are in cm.  Find the value of *x*.

x = ..................
[Total 4 marks]

**Exam Practice Tip**

It's a good idea to check your solutions by substituting them back into the equation and checking that everything works out properly. It certainly beats sitting and twiddling your thumbs or counting sheep for the last few minutes of your exam.

Score

13

# Formulas and Equations from Words

**1** A square has a side length of 3*x*.

a) Find a formula for the area, *A*, of the square in terms of *x*.

.................................................
[1]

b) The value of *x* is 4 cm. What is the area of the square?

........................ cm²
[1]
*[Total 2 marks]*

**2** The total cost for a group of people having afternoon tea at a hotel can be worked out using the following rule.

Multiply the number of people by 10. → Add on the number of items of food that were eaten in total. → Total cost in pounds.

a) Find a formula for the total cost of afternoon tea, *C* pounds, for *p* people eating a total of *e* items.

.................................................
[1]

b) If 4 people went for afternoon tea and ate 8 items each, what would be the total cost?

£ ............................
[2]
*[Total 3 marks]*

**3** Morgana and Iona are both travelling to London.

Morgana took the train. The train ticket for Morgana's journey would normally cost £*T*, but Morgana got it for half price because she had a railcard.

Iona took a taxi. The taxi fare costs £3 plus an extra 50p per mile.
Iona's journey was *d* miles long and she paid the same amount as Morgana.

a) Show that $3 + 0.5d = \dfrac{T}{2}$.

[1]

b) The taxi journey was 2 miles long.
How much would the train journey cost without a railcard?

£ ........................
[2]
*[Total 3 marks]*

Score: ☐
8

Section Two — Algebra

# Rearranging Formulas

**1** The formula $v = u + at$ can be used to calculate the speed of a car.

  a) Rearrange the formula to make $u$ the subject.

  ....................................
  *[1]*

  b) Rearrange the formula to make $t$ the subject.

  ....................................
  *[2]*
  *[Total 3 marks]*

**2** Rearrange the formula $\frac{a+2}{3} = b - 1$ to make $a$ the subject.

....................................
*[Total 2 marks]*

**3** Rearrange the formula $x = y^2 - 7$ to make $y$ the subject.

*Don't forget that a square root has two values — one positive and one negative.*

....................................
*[Total 2 marks]*

**4** Rearrange the formula $u = 2 + \frac{1}{w}$ to make $w$ the subject.

....................................
*[Total 3 marks]*

Score: ☐ / 10

Section Two — Algebra

# Quadratic Equations

**1** Fully factorise the expression $x^2 + 9x + 18$.

...................................
*[Total 2 marks]*

**2** Fully factorise the expression $y^2 - 4y - 5$.

$y^2 - 4y - 5 = (y + \text{.............})(y - \text{.............})$

...................................
*[Total 2 marks]*

**3** Fully factorise the expression $x^2 + 4x - 32$.

...................................
*[Total 2 marks]*

**4** The equation $x^2 - 9x + 20 = 0$ is an example of a quadratic equation.

a) Fully factorise the expression $x^2 - 9x + 20$.

...................................
*[2]*

b) Use your answer to part a) to solve the equation $x^2 - 9x + 20 = 0$.

$x = \text{.............}$ or $x = \text{.............}$
*[1]*

*[Total 3 marks]*

**5** Factorise $x^2 + 4x - 12$, and hence solve $x^2 + 4x - 12 = 0$.

$x = \text{.............}$ or $x = \text{.............}$
*[Total 3 marks]*

---

**Exam Practice Tip**

In the exam, you can check that you've factorised an expression properly by expanding the brackets back out. You should get the same expression that you started with. If you don't then something must have gone wrong somewhere down the line and you'll need to give it another go. Sorry about that.

**Score:** 12

# Trial and Improvement

**1** The equation $x^3 + 4x = 24$ has a solution between 2 and 3.

Use trial and improvement to find this solution.
Give your answer correct to 1 decimal place and show your working.

| $x$ | $x^3 + 4x$ | Notes |
|---|---|---|
| 2 | 16 | too small |
| 3 | .................. | too big |
| 2.5 | .................. | .................. |
| .......... | .................. | .................. |
| .......... | .................. | .................. |
| .......... | .................. | .................. |

$x = $ ..................

*[Total 4 marks]*

**2** A solution to the equation $x^3 + 5x - 12 = 0$ lies between 1 and 2.

Use trial and improvement to find this solution correct to 1 decimal place.
You must show all of your working.

$x = $ ..................

*[Total 4 marks]*

**3** The equation $x^2(x + 1) = 64$ has a solution between 3 and 4.

Find this solution correct to 1 decimal place.
Use the trial and improvement method and show your working.

$x = $ ..................

*[Total 4 marks]*

*Exam Practice Tip*
With trial and improvement questions it's really important that you write down all of your working in the exam. If you don't, the examiner won't be able to tell which method you've used and you'll probably end up losing marks... which would be sad, especially if you've gone to all the effort of getting the answer right.

Score: 12

# Sequences

**1** The $n$th term of a sequence is given by $3n + 2$.

What are the first three terms of this sequence?

................................................................
*[Total 2 marks]*

**2** The first four terms in a sequence are 3, 8, 13, 18, ...

a) Write down the next two terms in the sequence.

................................................................
*[1]*

b) Find the $n$th term of the sequence.

................................................................
*[2]*

c) What is the 30th term of the sequence?

................................................................
*[1]*

*[Total 4 marks]*

**3** Look at this sequence: 4, 6, 10, 16, 24...

a) Write down the next two terms in the sequence.

................................................................
*[2]*

b) The $n$th term of another sequence is $n^2 - n + 10$.
Find the 100th term in this sequence.

................................................................
*[1]*

*[Total 3 marks]*

Section Two — Algebra

**4** The patterns below are made up of grey and white squares.

Pattern 1   Pattern 2   Pattern 3   Pattern 4

a) Find an expression for the number of **grey** squares in the *n*th pattern.

..................................
*[2]*

b) In total, there is 1 square in the first pattern, 7 in the second, 17 in the third and 31 in the fourth. Which pattern will be the first to have more than 75 squares in total? Show all your working.

..................................
*[3]*
*[Total 5 marks]*

**5** A quadratic sequence begins 2, 6, 12, 20, …

a) Write down the next two terms in the sequence.

..................................
*[2]*

b) Find an expression for the *n*th term of the sequence.

..................................
*[3]*
*[Total 5 marks]*

**Exam Practice Tip**
Sequence questions are all about spotting the pattern — don't be put off if it's one you haven't come across before (like one involving roots or fractions). Shape sequences work just the same as number sequences once you work out how the shape changes from one pattern to the next.

Score

19

Section Two — Algebra

# Inequalities

**1**    $n$ is an integer. List all the possible values of $n$ that satisfy the inequality $-3 \leq n < 2$.

..................................................

*[Total 2 marks]*

**2**    Find the integer values of $p$ which satisfy the inequality $9 < 2p \leq 18$.

..................................................

*[Total 3 marks]*

**3**    Solve the following inequalities.

     a)    $6q - 8 < 40$

..................................................
*[2]*

     b)    $\dfrac{3x}{4} \leq 9$

..................................................
*[2]*

*[Total 4 marks]*

**4**    Solve the following inequalities.

     a)    $7x - 2 < 2x - 42$

..................................................
*[2]*

     b)    $9 - 4x > 17 - 2x$

..................................................
*[2]*

*[Total 4 marks]*

**5**    Solve the inequality $3 \leq 2p + 5 \leq 15$.

..................................................

*[Total 2 marks]*

Section Two — Algebra

**6** Find the integer values that satisfy **both** of the following inequalities:

$5n - 3 \leq 17$ and $2n + 6 > 8$

......................................................
[Total 4 marks]

**7** Look at the two cuboids below. The volume of cuboid B is greater than that of cuboid A.

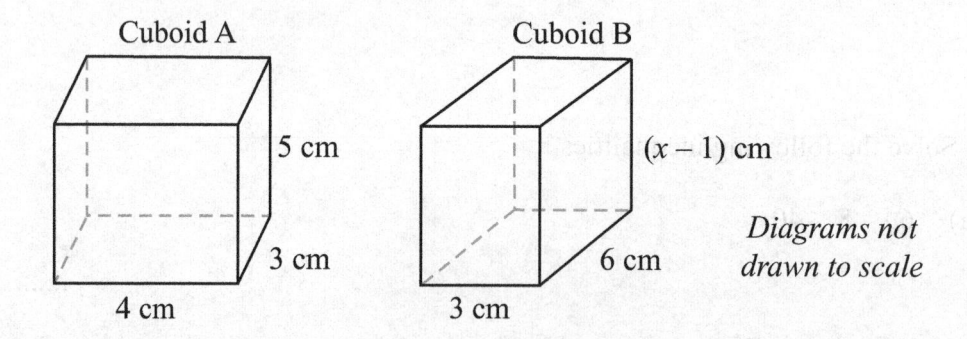

Cuboid A: 5 cm, 3 cm, 4 cm

Cuboid B: $(x - 1)$ cm, 6 cm, 3 cm

*Diagrams not drawn to scale*

The value of $x$ is a whole number. By forming and solving an inequality, find the smallest possible value of $x$.

*Marks will be awarded for the organisation, communication and written accuracy of your answer.*

......................................................
[5 + 2 OCW]
[Total 7 marks]

Score: ☐
26

Section Two — Algebra

# Simultaneous Equations

**1** Solve this pair of simultaneous equations.

$x + 3y = 11$
$3x + y = 9$

$x = $ .............  $y = $ .............
*[Total 4 marks]*

**2** A telephone mast is $l$ km from Llandudno and $c$ km from Colwyn Bay.

Llandudno is twice as far from the mast as Colwyn Bay is from the mast.
Colwyn Bay is 4 km closer to the mast than Llandudno is to the mast.

What is the distance between the telephone mast and each of Llandudno and Colwyn Bay?

Llandudno: ................ km    Colwyn Bay: ................ km
*[Total 3 marks]*

**3** Solve this pair of simultaneous equations.

$2x + 3y = 12$
$5x + 4y = 9$

$x = $ .............  $y = $ .............
*[Total 4 marks]*

**4** Two shapes, *ABCD* and *PQR*, are shown below.

Use the information in the diagram to find the values of $x$ and $y$.

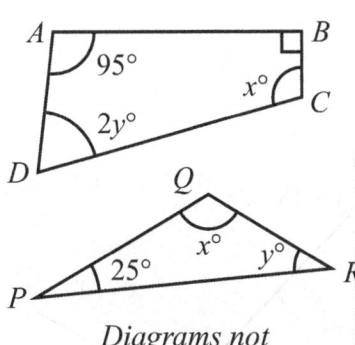

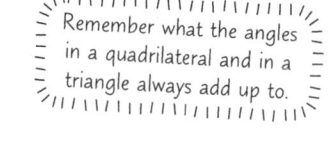

*Remember what the angles in a quadrilateral and in a triangle always add up to.*

ABCD: $A = 95°$, $B$ (right angle), $C = x°$, $D = 2y°$
PQR: $P = 25°$, $Q = x°$, $R = y°$

*Diagrams not drawn to scale*

$x = $ .............  $y = $ .............
*[Total 6 marks]*

### Exam Practice Tip
When you're solving simultaneous equations in the exam, it's always a good idea to check your answers at the end. Just substitute your values for x and y back into the original equations and see if they add up as they should. If they don't then you must have gone wrong somewhere, so go back and check your working.

Score: 17

Section Two — Algebra

# Solving Equations Using Graphs

**1** The diagram below shows graphs of $2y - x = 5$ and $4y + 3x = 25$.

Use the diagram to solve these simultaneous equations:
$2y - x = 5$
$4y + 3x = 25$

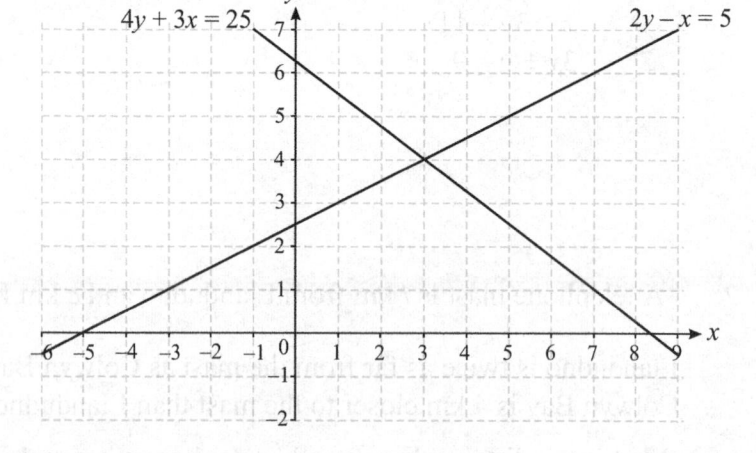

$x = $ ............ $y = $ ............

*[Total 1 mark]*

**2** The diagram below shows graphs of $y = x + 1$ and $y = 4 - 2x$.

a) Use the diagram to solve these simultaneous equations:
$y = x + 1$
$y = 4 - 2x$

$x = $ ............ $y = $ ............
*[1]*

b) By drawing another straight line, solve these simultaneous equations:
$y = x + 1$
$3y = x + 9$

$x = $ ............ $y = $ ............
*[2]*

*[Total 3 marks]*

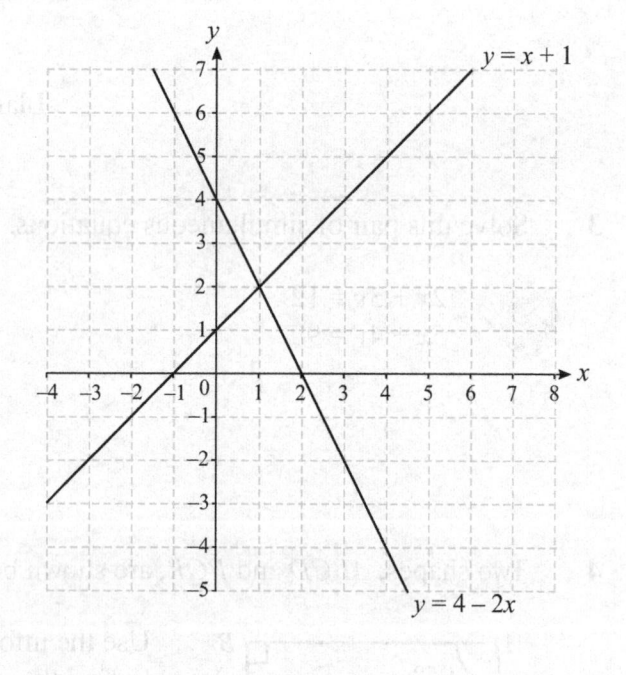

**3** The diagram shows graphs of $y = 18 - 3x$ and $y = 2x - 2$.

a) Find the coordinates of point $P$.

$P$ (................ , ................)
*[1]*

b) Find the coordinates of point $Q$.

$Q$ (................ , ................)
*[4]*

*[Total 5 marks]*

Section Two — Algebra

**4** The graph below shows $y = x^2 - 3x + 2$.

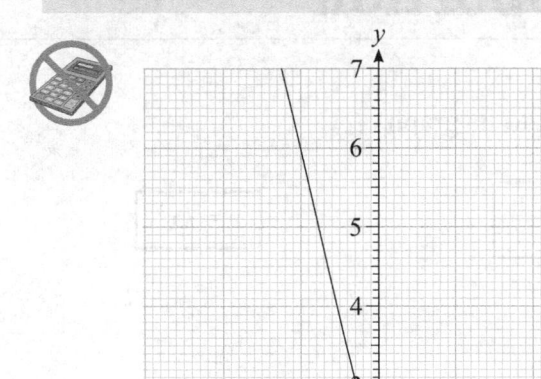

a) Find the values of $x$ when $x^2 - 3x + 2 = 0$.

$x = $ ..................

$x = $ ..................
*[1]*

b) Using the graph, find the solutions of $x^2 - 3x + 2 = 6$.

$x = $ ..................

$x = $ ..................
*[2]*

*[Total 3 marks]*

**5** The graph of the curve $y = x^2 - x - 4$ is shown below.

By drawing an appropriate line on the graph, determine the solutions to the equation $x^2 - x = 3$ correct to 1 decimal place.

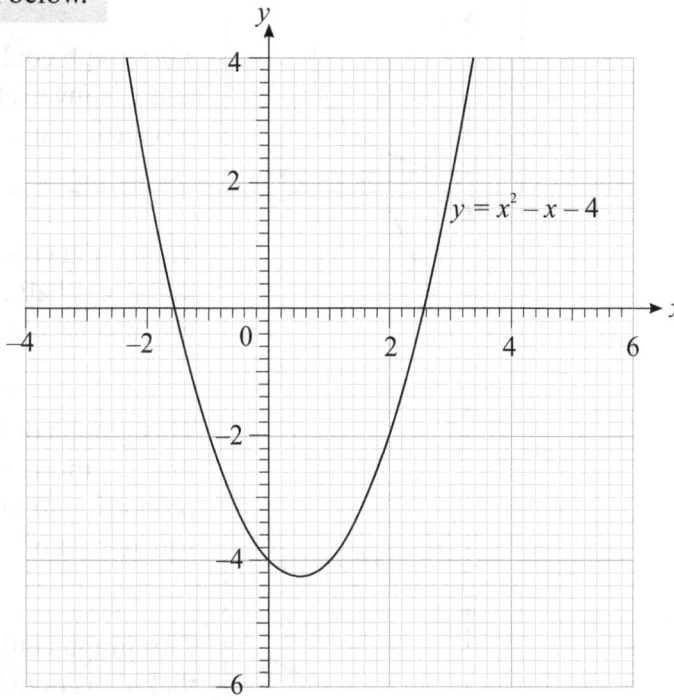

$x = $ ..................

$x = $ ..................

*[Total 3 marks]*

# Algebraic Proportion

**1** Draw a line connecting each proportionality statement to its graph.

| $y$ is directly proportional to $x$ | $y \propto \frac{1}{x}$ | $y = kx^3$ |

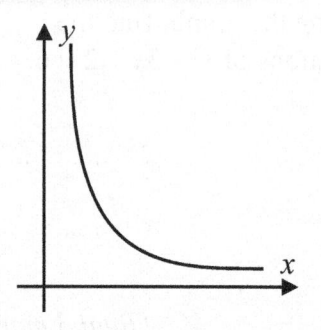

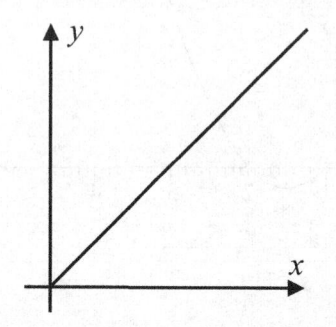

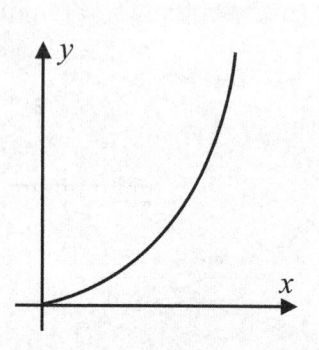

[Total 2 marks]

**2** Circle either true or false for each of the statements in this table.

| Graph | Statement | | |
|---|---|---|---|
| 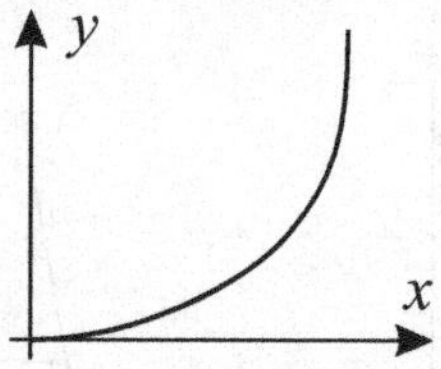 (graph) | This graph could show that $y$ is inversely proportion to $x^2$. | true | false |
| 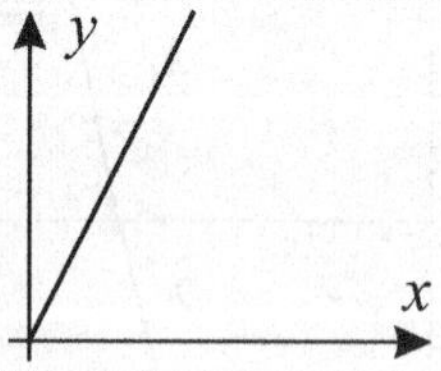 (graph) | This graph could show that if $x$ is halved then $y$ is also halved. | true | false |
| 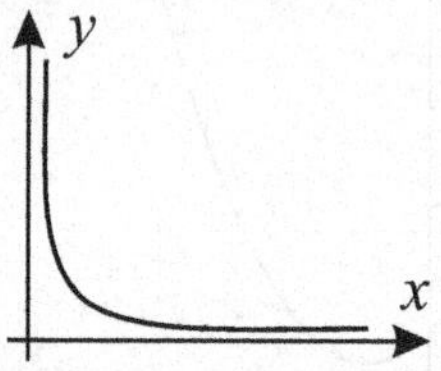 (graph) | This graph could show that $y$ is inversely proportion to the square root of $x$. | true | false |
| 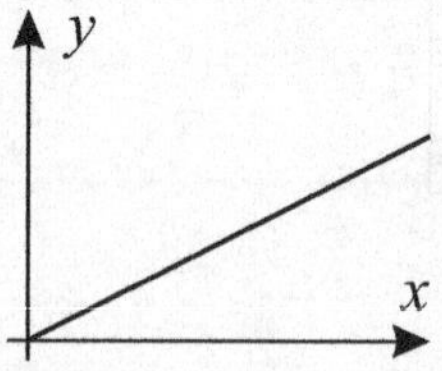 (graph) | This graph could show that if $x$ is doubled then $y$ is halved. | true | false |

[Total 2 marks]

Score: 4

Section Two — Algebra

# Coordinates and Midpoints

**1** Point *P* has coordinates (6, 2) and point *Q* has coordinates (–4, 1).

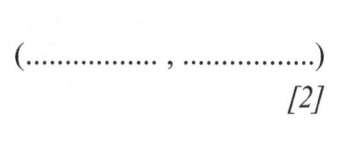

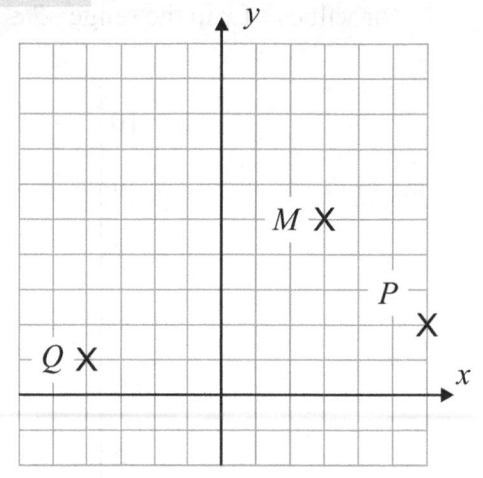

a) Find the coordinates of the midpoint of *PQ*.

(................. , .................)
*[2]*

b) Point *R* has coordinates (*a*, *b*).
The midpoint of *PR* is *M*(3, 5).
Find the values of *a* and *b*.

*a* = .................... *b* = ....................
*[2]*

*[Total 4 marks]*

**2** Line **L** has the equation $y = 2x - 3$ and passes through the points *A* (0, –3) and *B* (5, 7), as shown on the right.

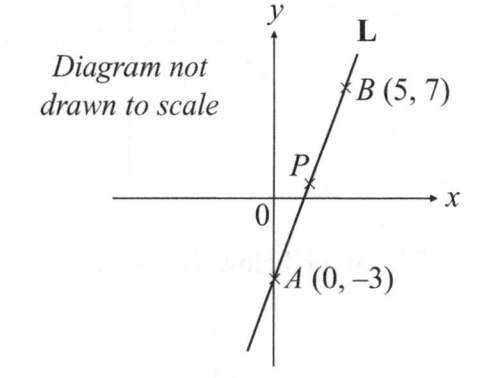

*Diagram not drawn to scale*

a) Find the coordinates of the point where **L** meets the *x*-axis.

(................. , .................)
*[1]*

b) Which of these sets of coordinates represents a point that lies on the line?
Circle your answer.

(2, –3)         (3, 3)         (–3, 3)         (2, –7)

*[1]*

c) Point *P* is the midpoint of the line segment *AB*.
Determine the coordinates of *P*.

*P* (................. , .................)
*[2]*

*[Total 4 marks]*

Score:

8

Section Two — Algebra

# Straight Lines

**1** Draw the graph $2y + x = 7$ on the axes below, for values of $x$ in the range $-2 \leq x \leq 10$.

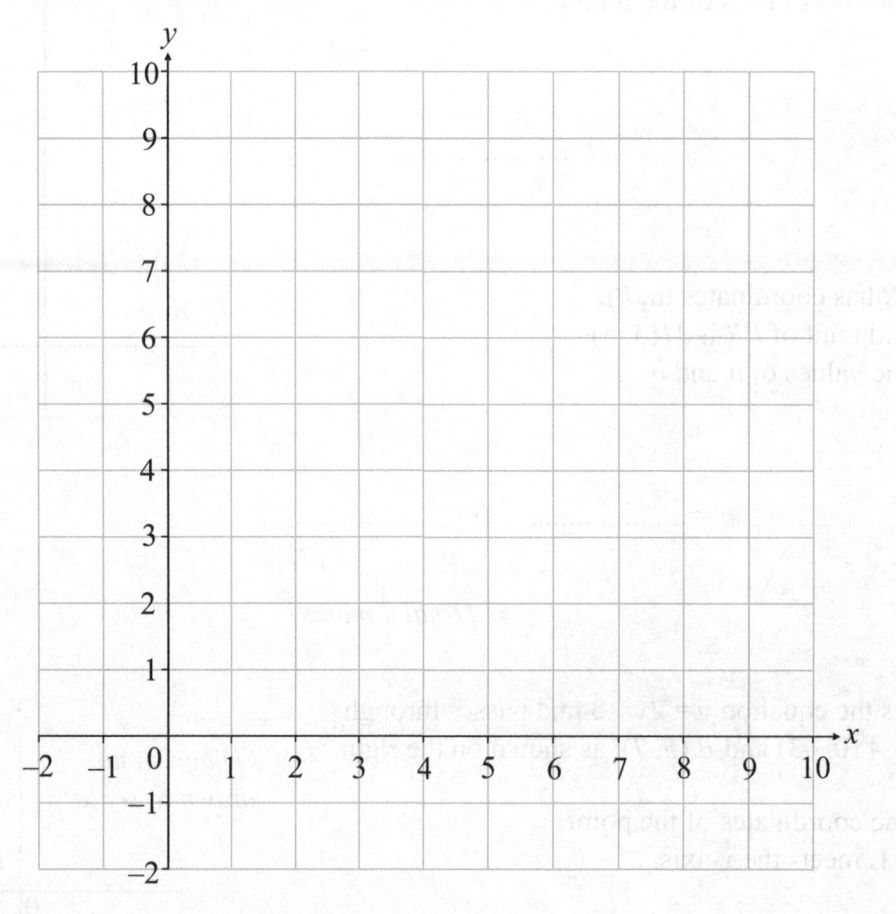

*[Total 1 mark]*

**2** The graph below shows 3 lines — **a**, **b** and **c**.

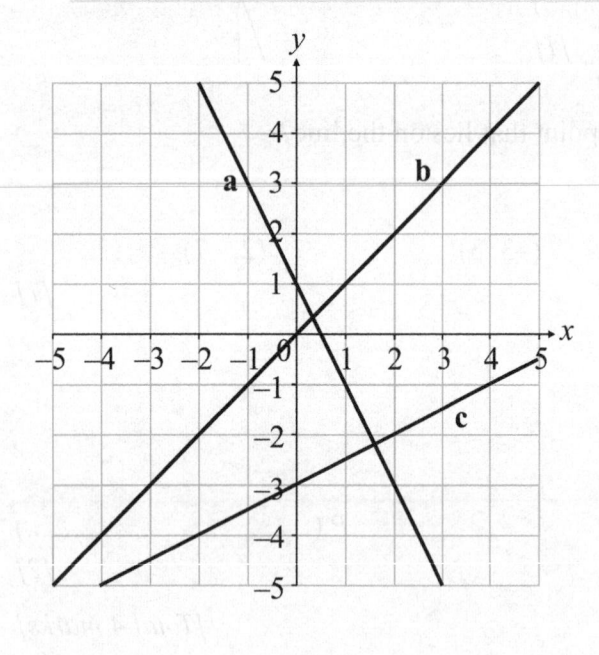

For each question below, circle the correct answer.

a) What is the gradient of line **a**?

$\quad 2 \qquad \dfrac{1}{2} \qquad -\dfrac{1}{2} \qquad -2$

*[1]*

b) Which of these lines is parallel to line **b**?

$\quad y = 2x \qquad\qquad y = x + 2$

$\quad y = -x \qquad\qquad y = 3x + 1$

*[1]*

c) Which of these lines is perpendicular to line **c**?

$\quad y = 2x - 3 \qquad\qquad y = -\dfrac{1}{2}x - 3$

$\quad y = -2x + 2 \qquad\qquad y = 2x + \dfrac{1}{3}$

*[2]*

*[Total 4 marks]*

Section Two — Algebra

**3** The line **M** passes through the points (–1, 17) and (5, –7).

a) Find the equation of **M**. Give your answer in the form $y = mx + c$.

..............................................
[3]

b) The line **W** is parallel to **M** and passes through the point (1, –3).
Find the equation of the line **W**. Give your answer in the form $y = mx + c$.

..............................................
[2]

[Total 5 marks]

**4** The graphs of two equations are sketched below. The equation of line **A** is $3x + 4y = 12$.

a) Find the gradient of line **A**.

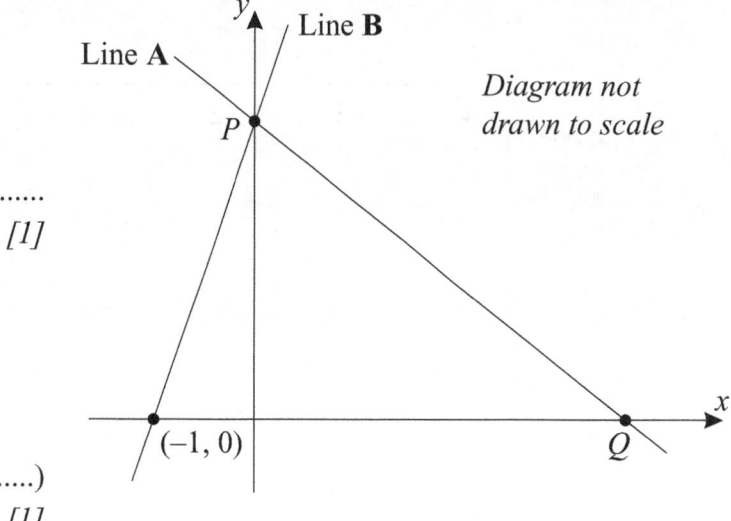

..............................................
[1]

b) Find the coordinates of point Q.

Q (..................,..................)
[1]

c) Given that both lines pass through point P on the y-axis, find the equation of line **B**.

..............................................
[3]

[Total 5 marks]

Score: ☐ / 15

Section Two — Algebra

# Quadratic Graphs

**1** This is a question about the function $y = x^2 + 2x - 5$.

a) Complete the table below.

| x | −4 | −3 | −2 | −1 | 0 | 1 | 2 |
|---|---|---|---|---|---|---|---|
| y | ......... | −2 | −5 | ......... | ......... | −2 | 3 |

[2]

*Check your calculation method by seeing if you can find the y-values given in the question.*

b) Use your table to draw the graph of $y = x^2 + 2x - 5$ on the grid, for values of x in the range $-4 \leq x \leq 2$.

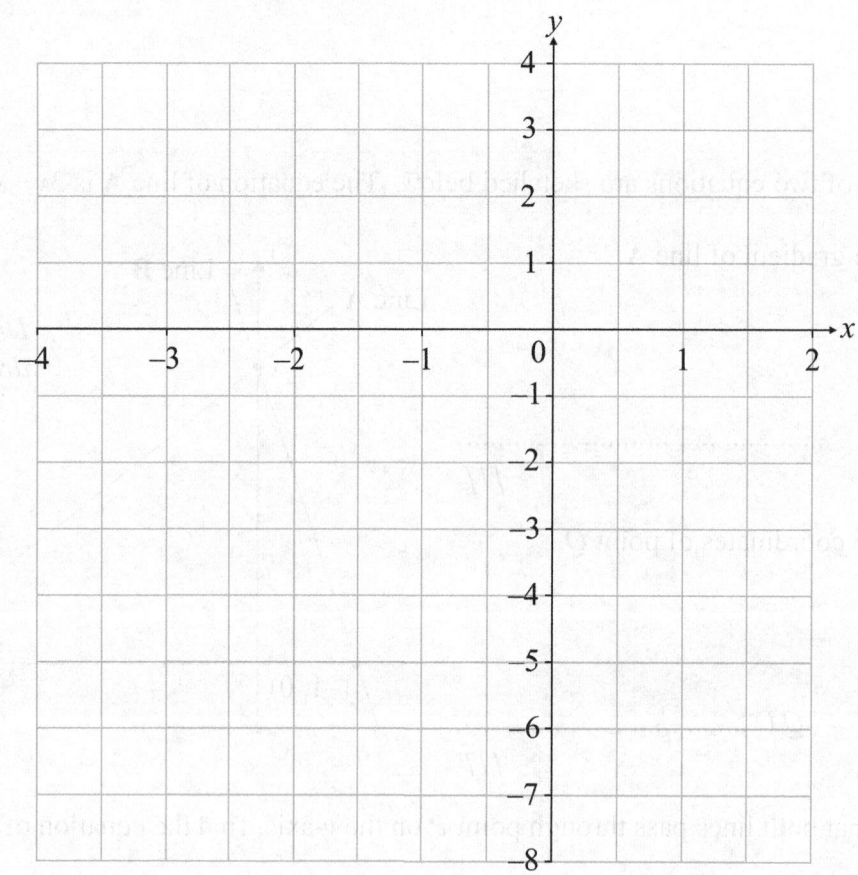

[2]

c) Draw the graph of $y = -1$ and then write down the x-values of the points where the graph of $y = -1$ intersects the curve $y = x^2 + 2x - 5$.

$x = $ .................... and $x = $ ....................

[2]

*[Total 6 marks]*

Section Two — Algebra

**2** Two variables are related by the equation $y = 32x - 4x^2$.

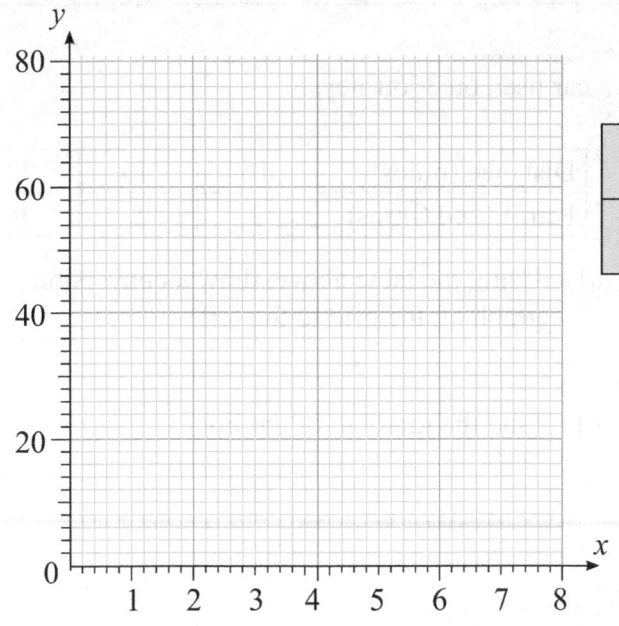

a) Find the value of $y$ for $x = 3$ and for $x = 4$ to complete the table below.

| $x$ | 0 | 1 | 2 | 3 | 4 | 5 | 6 | 7 | 8 |
|---|---|---|---|---|---|---|---|---|---|
| $y$ | 0 | 28 | 48 | ..... | ..... | 60 | 48 | 28 | 0 |

[2]

b) Draw the graph of $y = 32x - 4x^2$ for $0 \leq x \leq 8$ on the axes on the left.

[2]

c) Using the graph, give the coordinates of the highest point.

(................ , ................)
[1]
[Total 5 marks]

**3** Sketch the graph of $y = 2x^2 - 8$. Label with their coordinates the lowest point and any points where the curve intersects the axes.

[Total 3 marks]

**Exam Practice Tip**
If your curves aren't nice and smooth when you draw your quadratic graphs, you can be pretty sure you've gone wrong somewhere. Just take another look at your values and plot again. You could also solve these quadratic equations using algebra, but if the question asks you to use the graph, then make sure you use it.

Score

14

Section Two — Algebra

# Real-Life Graphs

**1** The table to the right shows how much petrol a car used on 3 journeys.

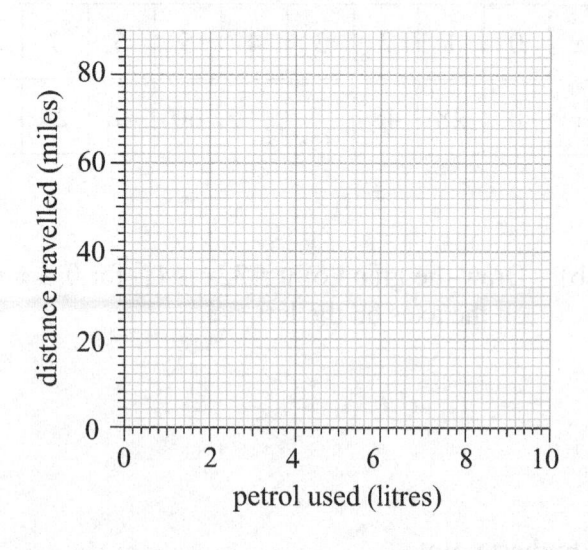

| Distance (miles) | 16 | 40 | 72 |
|---|---|---|---|
| Petrol used (litres) | 2 | 5 | 9 |

a) Using the table above, draw a conversion graph on the grid to the left.

[1]

b) Find the gradient of the line.

..................
[1]

c) What does the gradient of the line represent?

..........................................................................................................................
[1]

[Total 3 marks]

**2** An electricity company offers its customers two different price plans.

**Plan A:**
Monthly tariff of £18, plus 10p for each unit used.

**Plan B:**
No monthly tariff, just pay 40p for each unit used.

a) Use the graph to find the cost of using 70 units in a month for each plan.

Plan A .................. Plan B ..................
[2]

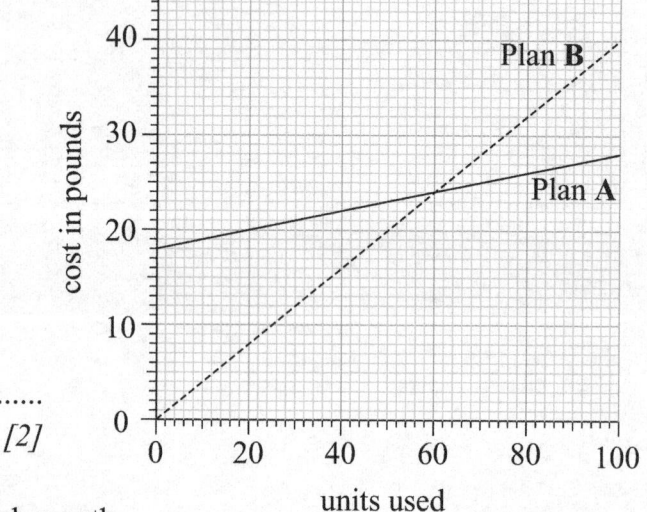

b) Mr Lloyd uses about 85 units of electricity each month. Which price plan would you advise him to choose? Explain your answer.

..........................................................................................................................

..........................................................................................................................
[2]

[Total 4 marks]

Score: 7

Section Two — Algebra

# Travel Graphs

**1** The distance-time graph below shows a 30 km running race between Rahul and Winifred.

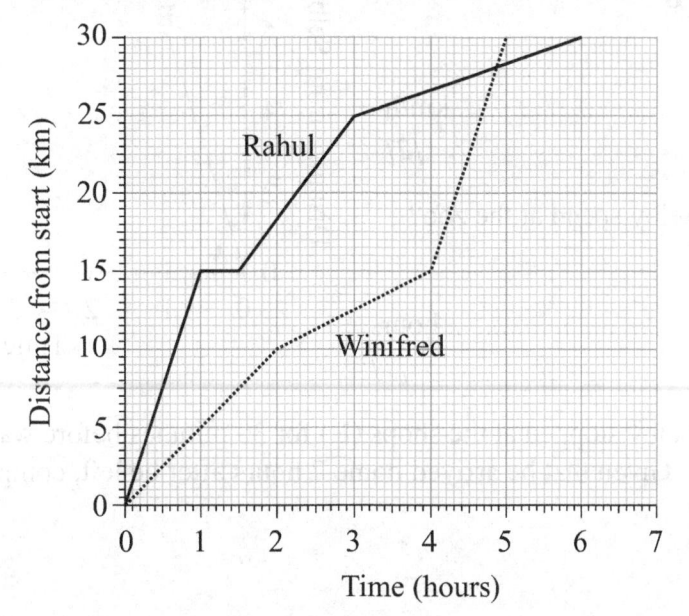

a) During the race, Rahul is stopped by a marshal.
After how many hours did he stop?

................ hours
*[1]*

b) Who won the race? How can you tell this from the graph?

...................................................................................................................................

...................................................................................................................................
*[1]*

c) What was Rahul's speed between 1.5 and 3 hours into the race?
Give your answer correct to 2 decimal places.

........................ km/h
*[2]*

d) During the race, one of the runners injured their leg.
Which runner do you think was injured?
What evidence is there on the graph to support your answer?

...................................................................................................................................

...................................................................................................................................

...................................................................................................................................
*[2]*

*[Total 6 marks]*

Section Two — Algebra

**2** The distance/time graph on the right shows Selby's journey from his house (**A**) to the zoo (**C**), which is 10 km away.

a) Calculate Selby's speed between **A** and **B**.

.......................... km/h
*[2]*

b) How long did Selby spend at the zoo?

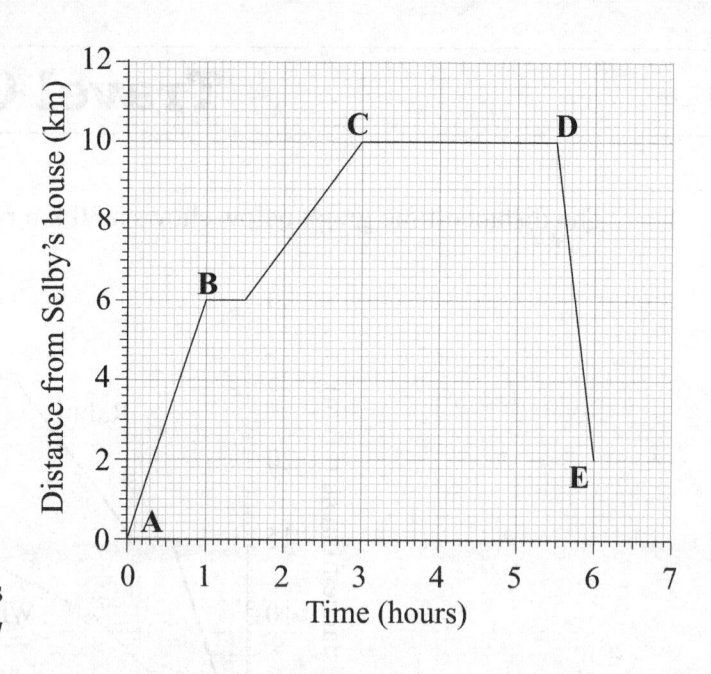

.......................... hours
*[1]*

c) After the zoo, Selby stopped at the shops (**E**) for 30 minutes before walking straight home at a constant speed. Given that he arrived home 7 hours after he left, complete the graph above.
*[2]*

*[Total 5 marks]*

**3** The velocity of a motorcycle is recorded over a minute.

a) Draw a velocity-time graph using the following information:
The motorcycle sets off from a standstill, accelerating at a constant rate for 10 seconds until it is moving at 10 m/s. It moves at a constant speed for the next 20 seconds.
The motorcycle then accelerates at a constant rate for 7 seconds until it is moving at 24 m/s. It moves at the same speed for 15 seconds before decelerating until it stops after 8 seconds.
*[3]*

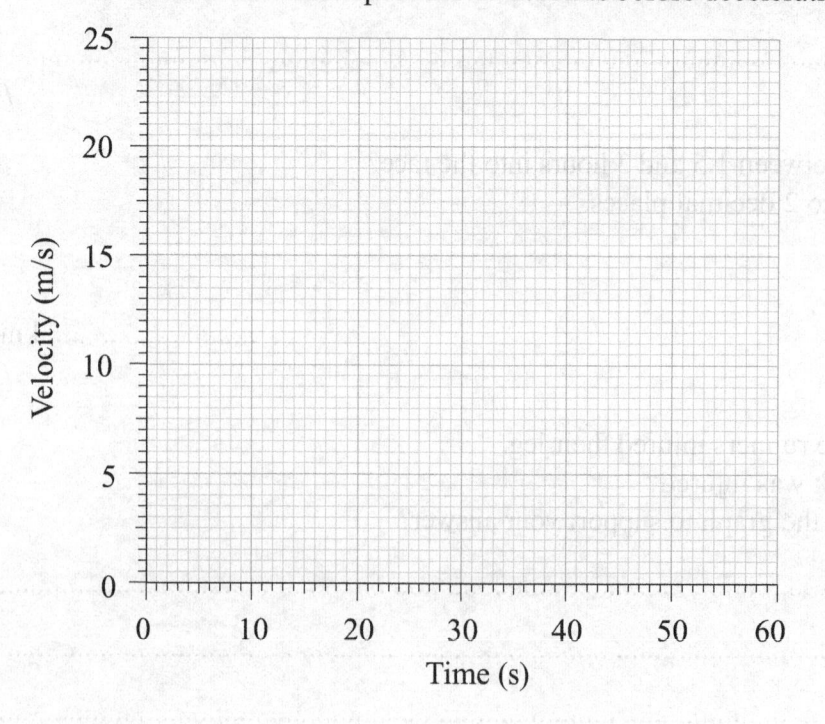

b) Calculate the acceleration of the motorcycle at 35 seconds.

.......................... m/s²
*[1]*

*[Total 4 marks]*

Section Two — Algebra

# Section Three — Geometry and Measure

## Symmetry

**1** Below is an image of a cog.

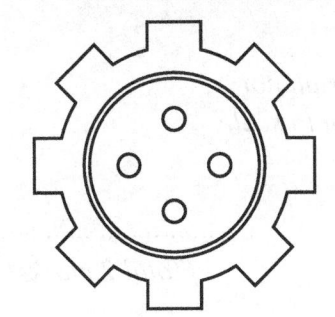

    a) Draw all the lines of symmetry for the cog. *[2]*

    b) What order of rotational symmetry does the cog have?

.................................
*[1]*

*[Total 3 marks]*

**2** Below is a pattern made by shading part of a square grid.

    a) How many lines of symmetry does the pattern have?

............................
*[1]*

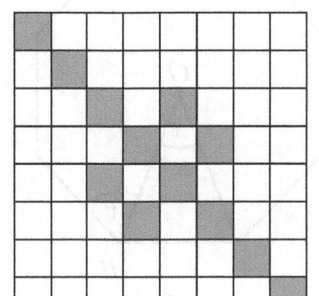

    b) What is the order of rotational symmetry of the pattern?

............................
*[1]*

*[Total 2 marks]*

**3** Shade one more square on each of the grids below to make:

    a) a shape with one line of symmetry.

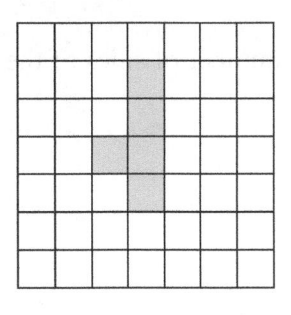

*[1]*

    b) a shape with rotational symmetry of order 2.

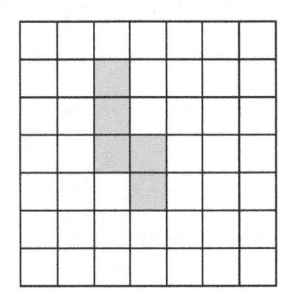

*[1]*

*[Total 2 marks]*

Score: 7

# Polygons

**1** Part of a regular polygon is shown below. The exterior angles of the polygon are 24°.

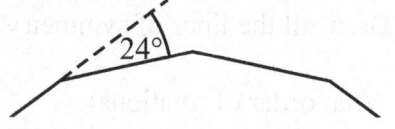

*Diagram not drawn to scale*

Work out the number of sides of the regular polygon.

.................................

*[Total 2 marks]*

**2** The diagram shows a regular octagon. AB is a side of the octagon and O is its centre.

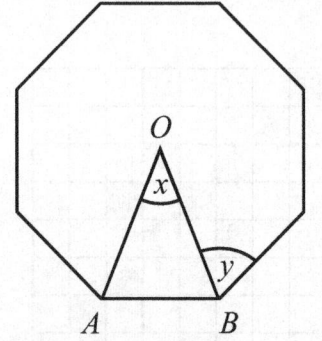

a) Work out the size of the angle marked x.

$x =$ ................. °

*[2]*

b) Work out the size of the angle marked y.

$y =$ ................. °

*[2]*

*Diagram not drawn to scale*

*[Total 4 marks]*

**3** Part of a regular polygon is shown on the right. Each interior angle is 150°.

Calculate the number of sides of the polygon.

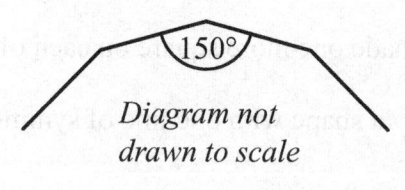

*Diagram not drawn to scale*

.................................

*[Total 3 marks]*

**4** A regular polygon has 18 sides. Explain whether or not this polygon will tessellate.

................................................................................................................

................................................................................................................

................................................................................................................

*[Total 3 marks]*

---

**Exam Practice Tip**

You need to make sure you learn those formulas about the exterior and interior angles of polygons — you won't be given them in the exam. And remember when you can use each one: two of them can be used for all polygons but the other two only apply to regular polygons (when all the sides and all the angles are the same).

**Score**

12

Section Three — Geometry and Measure

# Properties of 2D Shapes

**1** Circle the correct answer for each of the following questions.

a) What is the size of the reflex angle *LKN* on this diagram?

    40°        140°        220°        320°

*Diagram not drawn to scale*

[1]

b) Three angles in a trapezium are 90°, 90° and 45°. Which of these describes the fourth angle?

    obtuse        right-anged        acute        reflex

[1]

*[Total 2 marks]*

**2** One of the angles in a rhombus is 62°.

What are the sizes of its other three angles?

.............°, .............° and .............°

*[Total 2 marks]*

**3** An isosceles triangle has vertices *A*(1, 1), *B*(3, 7) and *C*(5, 1).

Give the equation of its line of symmetry.
Use the grid on the right to help you.

........................

*[Total 1 mark]*

**4** *ABCD* is a kite. *X* is the point where the diagonals *AC* and *BD* intersect.
Angle *ADC* = 75°.

a) Write down the size of angle *AXD*.

........................°

[1]

b) Ceri says, "Angle *ABC* must also be 75°." Do you agree? Explain your answer.

................................................................................................................................

................................................................................................................................

[2]

*[Total 3 marks]*

Score: 8

Section Three — Geometry and Measure

# Congruence and Similarity

**1** Look at the shapes on the right.

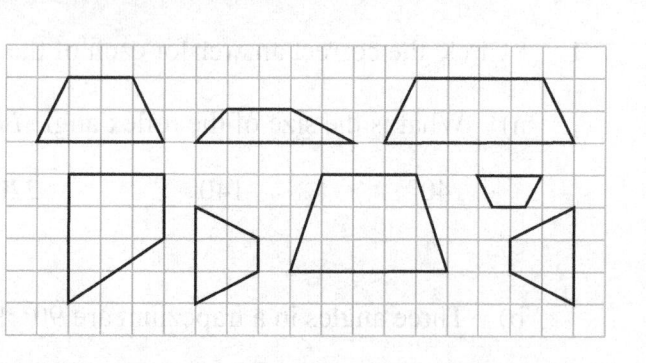

a) Write C in the two shapes that are **congruent**.
[1]

b) Write S in the two shapes that are **similar** but not congruent.
[1]

[Total 2 marks]

**2** The shapes ABCD and EFGH are mathematically similar.

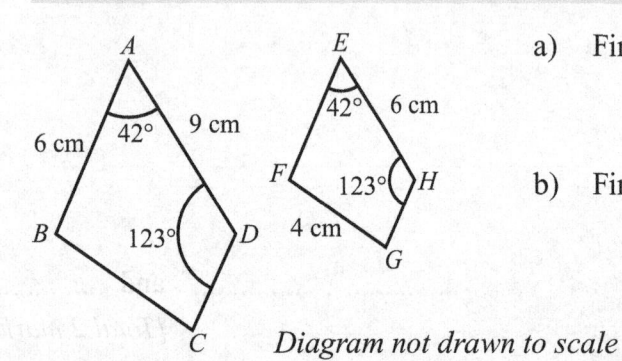

a) Find the length of EF.

................. cm
[2]

b) Find the length of BC.

................. cm
[1]

[Total 3 marks]

*Diagram not drawn to scale*

**3** Triangles ABC and DBE are similar. ABE and CBD are both straight lines.

Find the missing values $x$ and $y$.

*You'll need to use the rule about vertically opposite angles.*

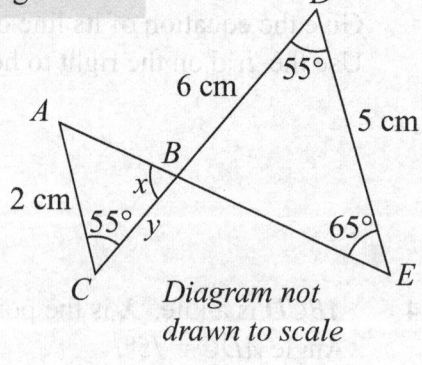

$x =$ ................°

$y =$ ................ cm

[Total 3 marks]

*Diagram not drawn to scale*

**4** Are triangles ABC and DEF congruent? Explain your answer.

*Start by finding one of the unknown side lengths.*

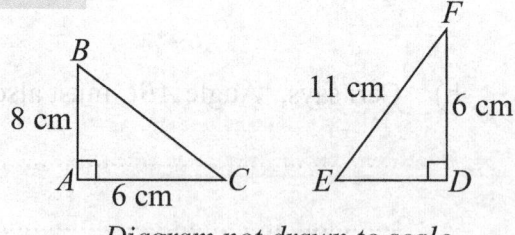

*Diagram not drawn to scale*

[Total 3 marks]

Score: ☐
11

# The Four Transformations

**1** Triangle **A** has been drawn on the grid below.

Reflect triangle **A** in the *y*-axis.
Label your image **B**.

*[Total 1 mark]*

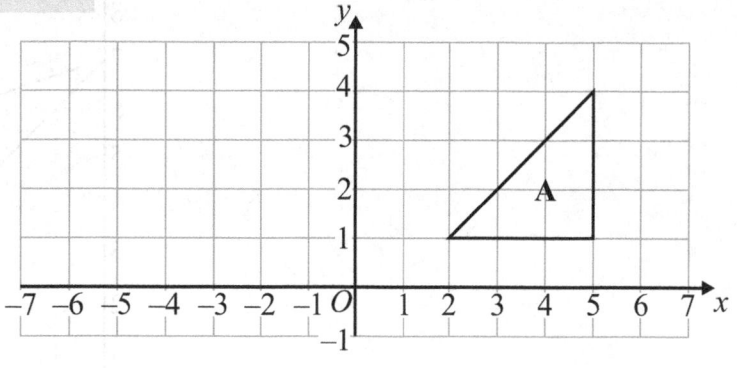

**2** Parallelogram **P** has been drawn on the grid below.

Enlarge parallelogram **P** with centre (6, –3) and scale factor 3.
Label your image **Q**.

*[Total 3 marks]*

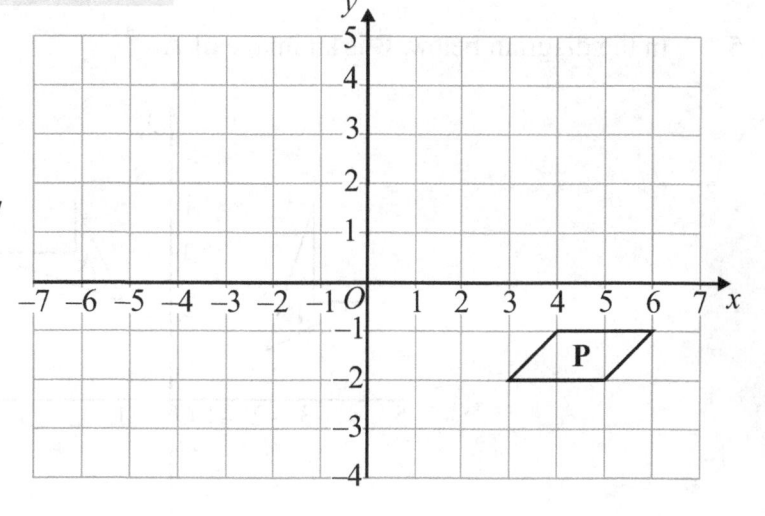

**3** Shapes **F** and **G** have been drawn on the grid below.

a) Write down the vector which describes the translation that maps **F** onto **G**.

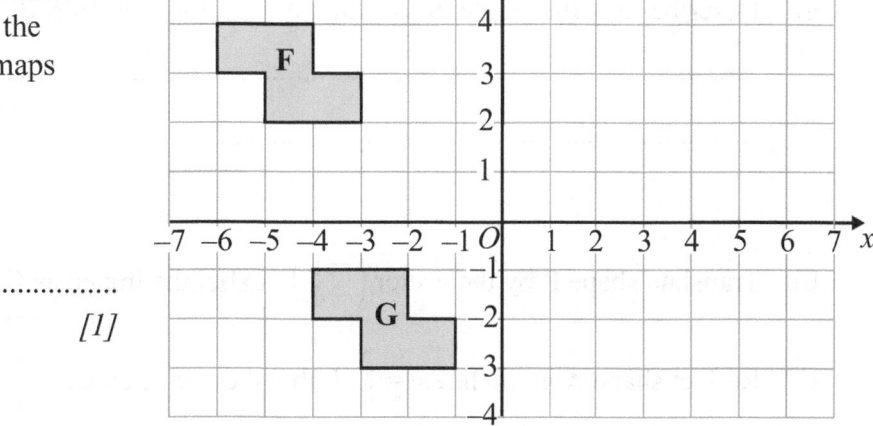

................
*[1]*

b) Rotate shape **F** by 90° clockwise around the point (0, –2).
Label your image **H**.

*[2]*

*[Total 3 marks]*

Section Three — Geometry and Measure

4   Triangle **S** has been drawn on the grid below.

Enlarge triangle **S** by scale factor $\frac{1}{2}$ with centre of enlargement (–6, 1). Label your image **T**.

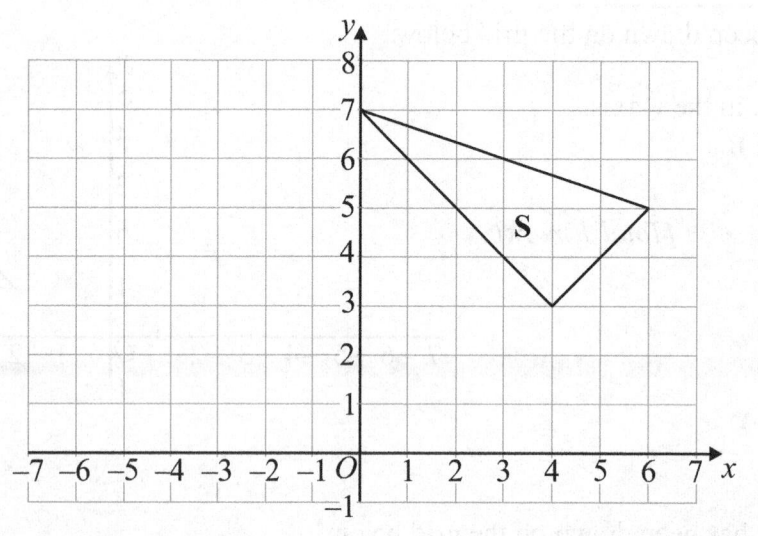

*[Total 3 marks]*

5   In the diagram below, **B** is an image of **A**.

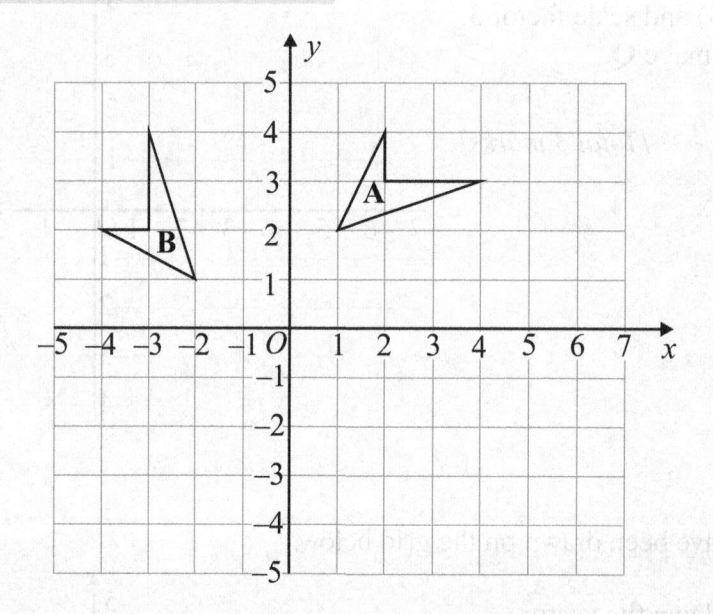

a) Describe fully the single transformation that maps **A** onto **B**.

................................................................................................................................

................................................................................................................................

*[3]*

b) Translate shape **B** by the vector $\begin{pmatrix} -1 \\ -4 \end{pmatrix}$. Label the image as **C**.

*[1]*

c) Reflect shape **A** in the line $y = 1$. Label the image as **D**.

*[2]*

*[Total 6 marks]*

Section Three — Geometry and Measure

# More Transformation Stuff

**1** Shape **A** has been drawn on the grid below.

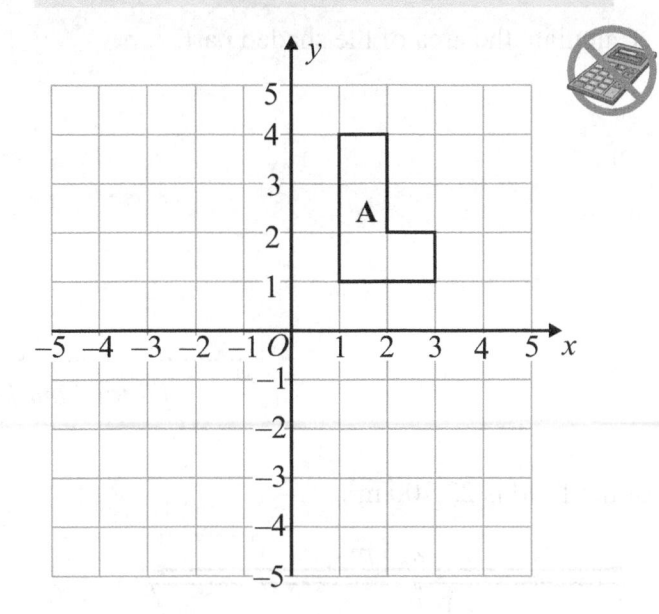

a) On the grid, reflect shape **A** in the *x*-axis. Label this image **B**.
[1]

b) Rotate shape **B** 90° clockwise about the origin. Label this image **C**.
[2]

c) Describe fully the single transformation which maps **A** onto **C**.

..................................................................

..................................................................

..................................................................
[2]

[Total 5 marks]

**2** Triangle **R** has been drawn on the grid below.

Reflect triangle **R** in the line $y = x$ and then enlarge it with centre (6, −3) and scale factor 3. Label the resulting shape **S**.

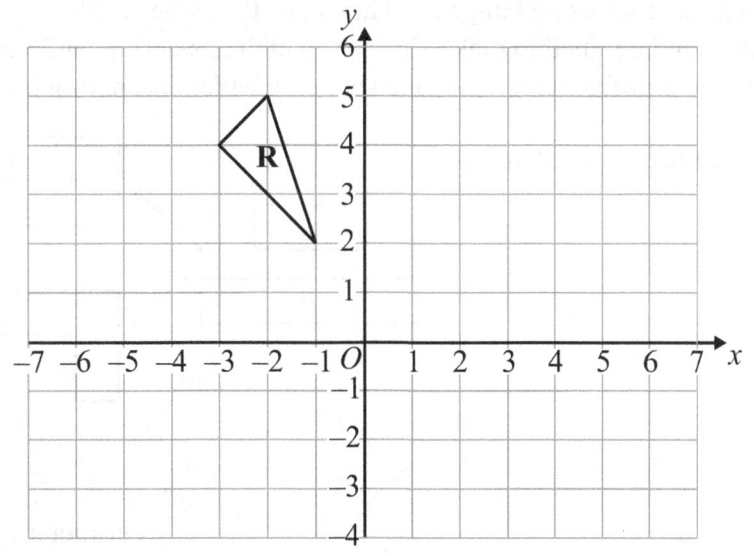

[Total 4 marks]

**Exam Practice Tip**

Remember — the four transformations are translation, rotation, reflection and enlargement. Make sure you're clear about what each transformation does and the details you need to describe them or carry them out. If the image of a transformation doesn't look like any of these, it might be the result of a combination of them.

Score

9

Section Three — Geometry and Measure

# Perimeter and Area

**1** The diagram below shows a rectangle with a right-angled triangle inside.

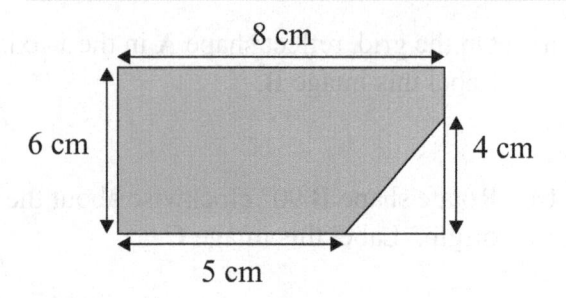

Calculate the area of the shaded part.

8 cm
6 cm
4 cm
5 cm

*Diagram not drawn to scale*

.......................... cm²

[Total 3 marks]

**2** The diagram below shows a field. The area of the field is 23 700 m².

Work out the value of $x$.

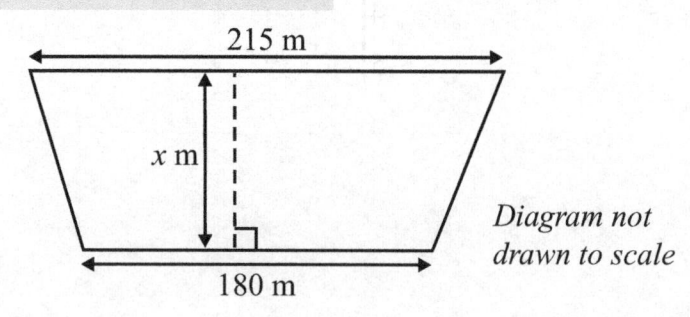

215 m
$x$ m
180 m

*Diagram not drawn to scale*

..........................

[Total 3 marks]

**3** Rectangle $B$ is twice as long as rectangle $A$. They have the same width.
The two rectangles can be joined to make shape $C$, which has perimeter 28 cm.
They can be joined in a different way to make shape $D$, which has perimeter 34 cm.

Find the perimeters of rectangles $A$ and $B$.

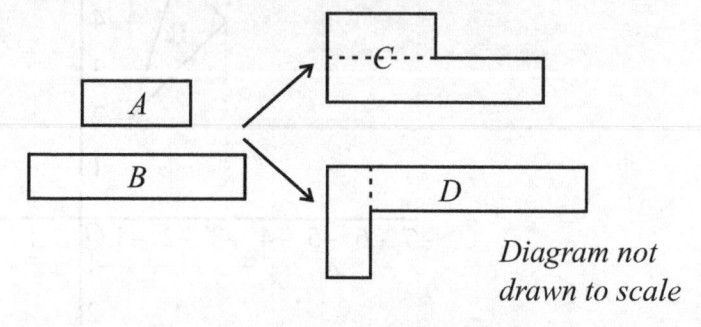

*Diagram not drawn to scale*

Perimeter of $A$: ..................... cm

Perimeter of $B$: ..................... cm

[Total 6 marks]

Score:

12

Section Three — Geometry and Measure

# Area — Circles

**1** A letter "O" is formed by cutting a circular section from the centre of a circular piece of card.

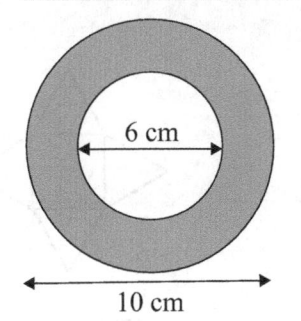

The diameter of the circle cut out is 6 cm.
The diameter of the circular card is 10 cm.

Calculate the area of the shaded region of the letter "O".
Give your answer correct to 3 significant figures.

*Diagram not drawn to scale*

.......................... cm²
*[Total 3 marks]*

**2** The diagram below shows a square with a circle inside.
The circle touches each of the four sides of the square.

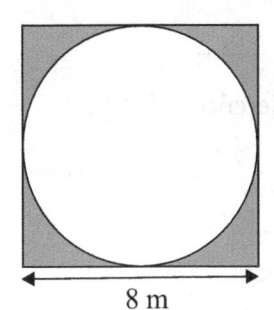

Calculate the shaded area. Give your answer correct to 2 decimal places.

....................... m²
*[Total 3 marks]*

**3** Lynn is designing a garden. The diagram shows her design.
Lynn's garden will be rectangular, with a semicircular flowerbed at one end, and a matching semicircular patio at the other end. The rest of the space will be taken up by a lawn.

The grass seed that Lynn is planning to use comes in boxes that cost £7 each. Each box will cover 10 m².

How much will it cost Lynn to cover the lawn with grass seed?

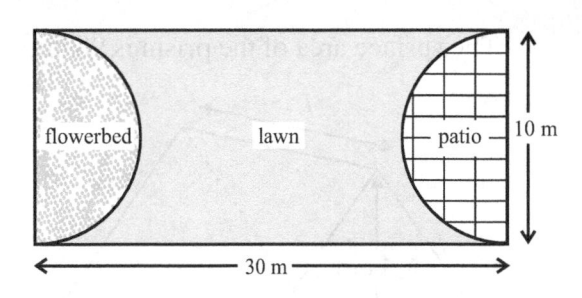

*Diagram not drawn to scale*

£ ......................
*[Total 4 marks]*

Score: 

**10**

Section Three — Geometry and Measure

# Nets and Surface Area

**1** Circle the net that makes a tetrahedron.

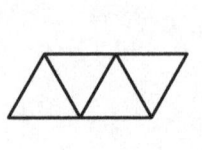

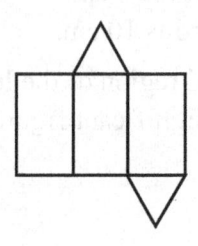

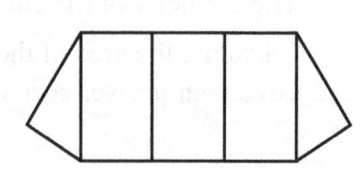

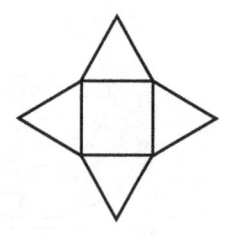

*[Total 1 mark]*

**2** The diagram below shows a cylinder.

Calculate the surface area of the cylinder. Give your answer in cm² correct to 3 significant figures.

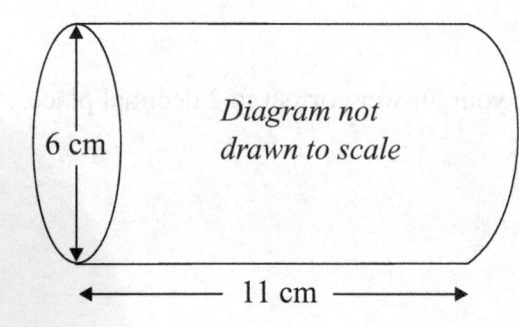

6 cm
*Diagram not drawn to scale*
11 cm

Area of cross-section = π × .............. = ..............

Circumference = π × .............. = ..............

Area of curved surface = circumference × length

= .............. × .............. = ..............

Total surface area = ( 2 × .............. ) + .............. = ..............

.......................... cm²
*[Total 4 marks]*

**3** The diagram below shows a triangular prism.
The triangular faces of the prism are equilateral triangles.

The surface area of the prism is 98 cm². Find the value of $l$, the length of the prism.

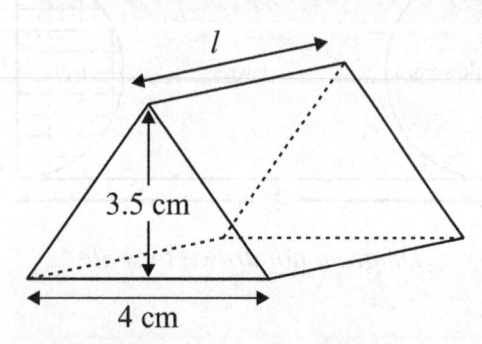

$l$
3.5 cm
4 cm
*Diagram not drawn to scale*

$l$ = ..................... cm
*[Total 4 marks]*

**Exam Practice Tip**
Nets are super useful in calculating the surface area of a 3D shape because they show you every face the shape has. Remember — some shapes have their own formula for working out the surface area, while for other shapes you need to work out the surface area of each face and add these up together.

Score: 9

# 3D Shapes — Volume

**1** The diagram below shows a prism with a trapezium as its cross-section.

What is the volume of the prism?

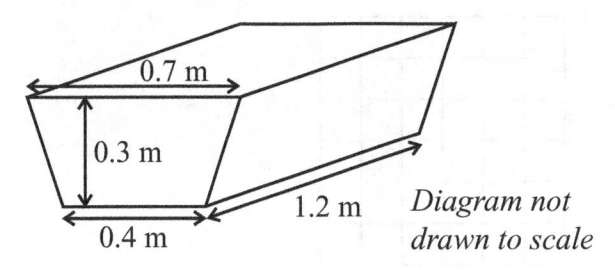

0.7 m
0.3 m
0.4 m
1.2 m
*Diagram not drawn to scale*

.................... m³
*[Total 2 marks]*

**2** The tank shown in the diagram below is completely filled with water.

a) Calculate the volume of water in the tank.

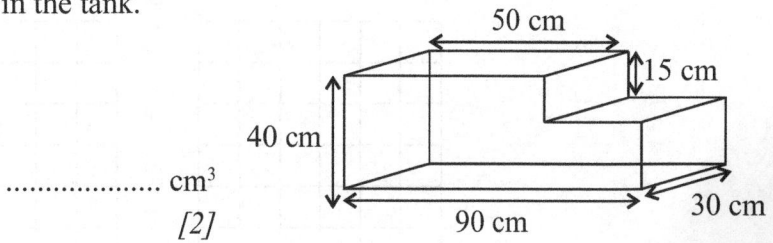

50 cm
15 cm
40 cm
90 cm
30 cm

.................... cm³
*[2]*

b) The water from this tank is then poured into a second tank, in the shape of a single cuboid, with length 120 cm. The depth of the water is 15 cm. What is the width of the second tank?

.................... cm
*[2]*

*[Total 4 marks]*

**3** The diagram below shows a new paddling pool. It has a diameter of 2 metres, and is 40 cm high.

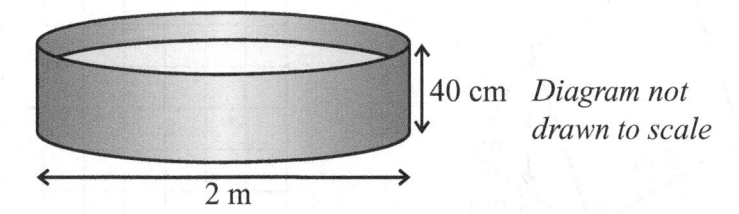

40 cm  *Diagram not drawn to scale*
2 m

The instructions that came with the pool say that it should only be filled three-quarters full.
What is the maximum volume of water that can be put in the pool?
Give your answer correct to 2 decimal places.

.................... m³
*[Total 3 marks]*

Score: 

9

Section Three — Geometry and Measure

# Projections

**1** The diagram below shows a solid made from identical cubes. The side elevation of the solid is drawn on the adjacent grid.

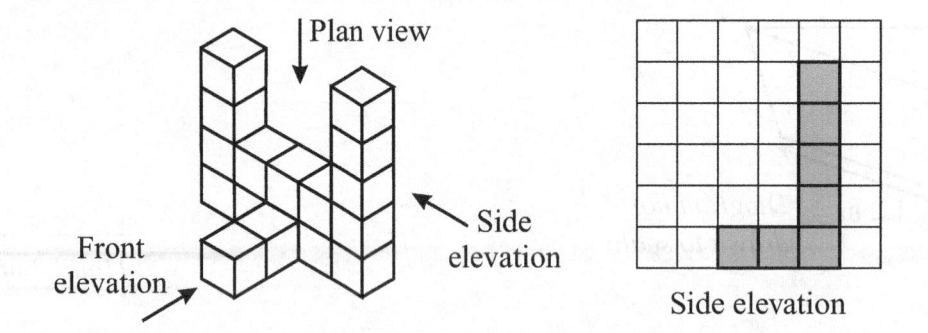

a) On the grid below, draw the front elevation of the solid. *[1]*

b) On the grid below, draw the plan view of the solid. *[1]*

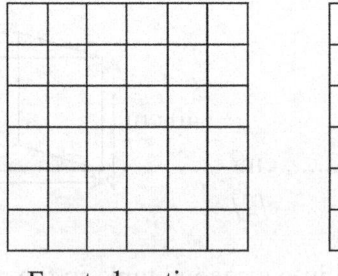

Front elevation

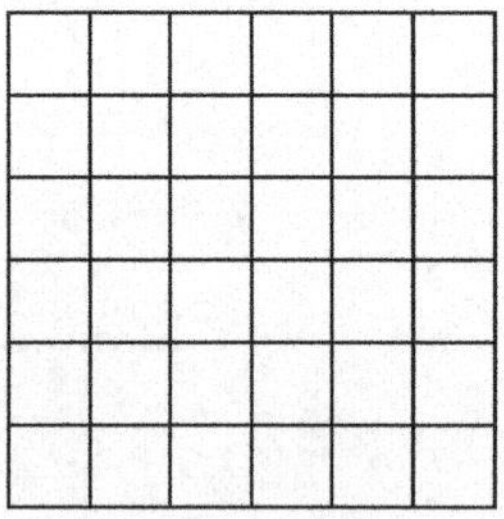

Plan view

*[Total 2 marks]*

**2** The diagram shows a house made of a 5 m × 5 m × 6 m cuboid and a triangular roof of width 4 m, length 5 m and vertical height 4 m.

On the grid below, draw the front elevation of the house. Use a scale of 1 square = 1 m.

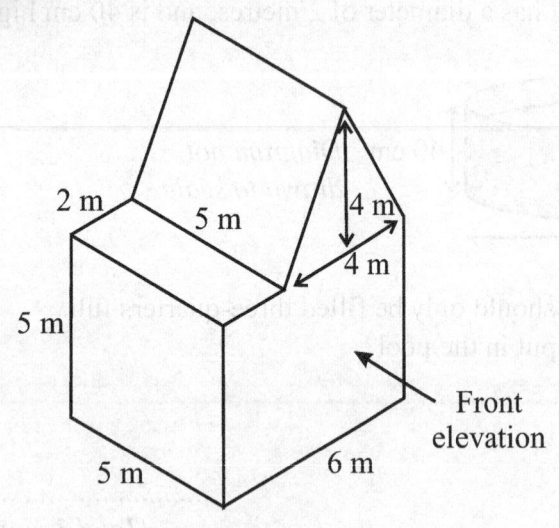

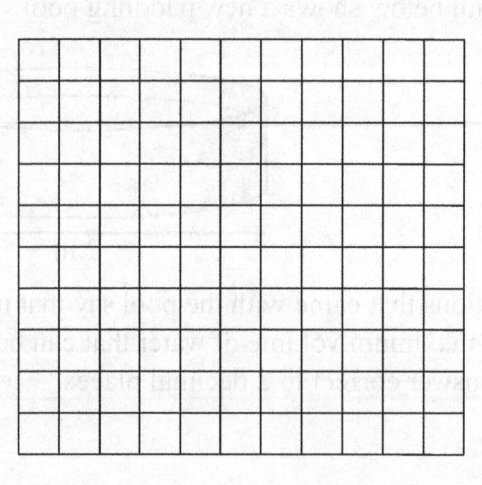

*[Total 2 marks]*

Score:

4

Section Three — Geometry and Measure

# Conversions

**1** Part of the bus timetable from Coventry to Rugby is shown on the right.

| Coventry | 14:45 | 16:15 | 17:45 |
| Bubbenhall | – | 16:40 | 18:10 |
| Birdingbury | – | 17:04 | – |
| Rugby | 15:35 | 17:30 | 18:40 |

a) Manon is travelling to Rugby. She leaves her house at 14:20 and it takes her 30 minutes to walk to the bus stop at Coventry. How long will it take her to get from her home to Rugby?

*The dashes on the timetable mean the bus doesn't stop.*

.................. hours .................. minutes
*[2]*

The 16:15 bus from Coventry continues to Lutterworth after Rugby. It arrives in Lutterworth at 18:15.

b) If Anne catches this bus from Bubbenhall, how many minutes will it take her to get to Lutterworth?

.................. minutes
*[2]*

*[Total 4 marks]*

**2** Gethin has just competed in a long jump competition. His best jump measured 9.5 feet. The winner's best jump was 4.6 m.

What is the difference, in cm, between Gethin's jump and the winner's jump? You may use the conversion 1 foot ≈ 30 cm.

.............................. cm
*[Total 3 marks]*

**3** The playing surface of a snooker table has an area of 39 200 cm².

Convert the area of the snooker table into m².

.............................. m²
*[Total 2 marks]*

**4** A barrel of oil has a capacity of 150 litres.

How many cubic metres of oil does the barrel hold?

.............................. m³
*[Total 3 marks]*

Section Three — Geometry and Measure

**5** Adil has a choice of two cars to hire for a holiday.
He wants to hire the most efficient car.

Car A will do 51.4 miles per gallon of petrol. Car B uses 6.2 litres of petrol per 100 km.
Which car should Adil hire? You may use the conversion 1 gallon ≈ 4.5 litres.

*To compare the cars, you need to convert one of their fuel efficiencies so they're both in the same units.*

......................................
*[Total 3 marks]*

**6** A cake has to be baked for 2¼ hours plus 10 minutes for every 100 g the cake weighs.

a) Mary put a 400 g cake in the oven at 9.55 am.
What time should Mary take the cake out of the oven?

......................................
*[3]*

b) Huw's cake needs to be baked for 195 minutes. Estimate the weight of his cake in pounds.

.......................... lb
*[3]*

*[Total 6 marks]*

**7** Here are some expressions. The letters $r$, $s$ and $t$ represent lengths.

$s^2 + 4t^2$        $s(s - r^2)$        $2rt^2$        $3(\pi r + t)$        $t(s^2 + 1)$

Write down one expression from the list above that could represent:

a) a length

......................................
*[1]*

b) an area

......................................
*[1]*

c) a volume

......................................
*[1]*

*[Total 3 marks]*

Score: 24

# Compound Measures

1   A land mass of 50 000 km² has a population of 17.5 million people.

   What is the population density? Circle the correct answer.

   250 population per km²        350 population per km²        450 population per km²

   *[Total 1 mark]*

2   The mass of a metal statue is 360 kg.
   The density of the metal alloy from which it is made is 1800 kg/m³.

   a)   Calculate the volume of the statue.

   ............................... m³
   *[2]*

   b)   It is decided that the metal alloy used is not resistant enough to wear and tear so it is replaced with another that has a density of 2700 kg/m³. The volume of the statue must remain the same. Calculate the mass of the new statue.

   ............................... kg
   *[2]*

   *[Total 4 marks]*

3   Adam has been caught speeding by a pair of average speed cameras. The speed limit was 50 mph.

   The cameras are 2500 m apart. The time taken for his car to pass between them was 102 seconds.

   a)   What was Adam's average speed between the cameras?
        Give your answer correct to the nearest mph.

   ........................ mph
   *[3]*

   b)   If Adam had been travelling within the speed limit, what is the minimum time it should have taken him to pass between the cameras? Give your answer correct to the nearest second.

   ............................... s
   *[2]*

   *[Total 5 marks]*

**Exam Practice Tip**
Formula triangles are a great way of remembering compound measures — just cover up the thing you want to find, write down what's left, put in the numbers and voilà, you've got yourself an answer. But make sure the measurements are in the right units before doing the calculation to avoid any awkward conversions later.

Score: 10

Section Three — Geometry and Measure

# Angles and Shapes

**1** ABC is an isosceles triangle, AB = BC and ACD is a straight line.

Work out the size of angle BCD.

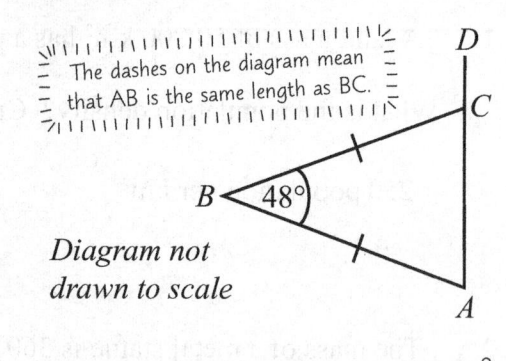

*The dashes on the diagram mean that AB is the same length as BC.*

*Diagram not drawn to scale*

.................................°

*[Total 3 marks]*

**2** BCD is a triangle. ABD is a straight line.

a) Find the value of x.

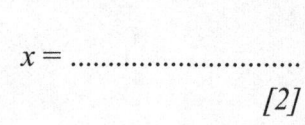

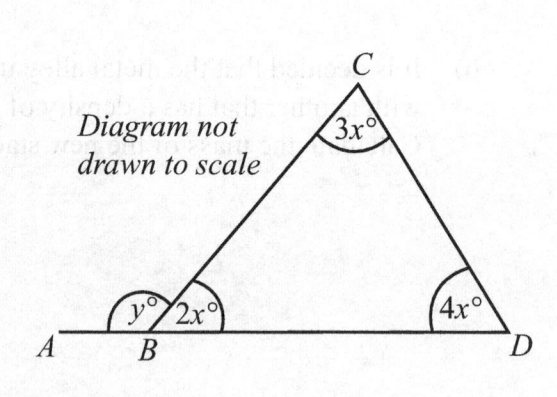

*Diagram not drawn to scale*

x = ..............................
*[2]*

b) Find the value of y.

y = ..............................
*[2]*

*[Total 4 marks]*

**3** BCDE is a quadrilateral with angle CDE = 90°. ABE is a straight line.

*Diagram not drawn to scale*

Work out the size of the angle marked x.

x = ..............................°

*[Total 3 marks]*

Section Three — Geometry and Measure

**4** *DEF* and *BEC* are straight lines that cross at *E*.
*AFB* and *AC* are perpendicular lines.

a) Find angle *x*.

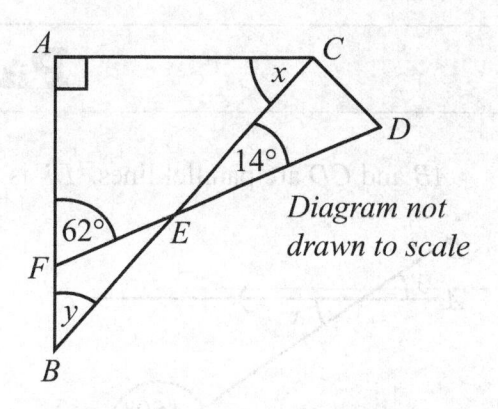

*Diagram not drawn to scale*

$x = $ .................................°

[2]

b) Hence explain why *y* = 48°.

..................................................................................................................................

..................................................................................................................................

[1]

[Total 3 marks]

**5** *ACDH* is a quadrilateral. *BCDE*, *GHD* and *AHF* are straight lines.

Work out the size of the angle marked *x*.

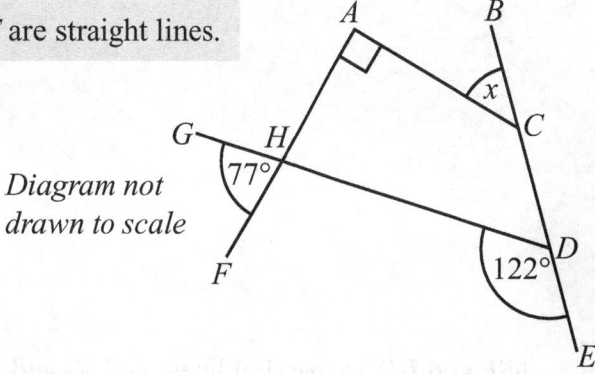

*Diagram not drawn to scale*

$x = $ .................................°

[Total 4 marks]

**6** Show that the triangle below is isosceles.

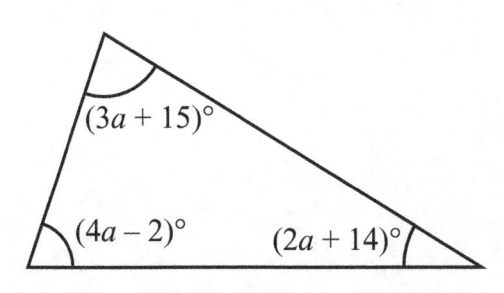

$(3a + 15)°$

$(4a - 2)°$     $(2a + 14)°$

*Diagram not drawn to scale*

[Total 5 marks]

**Exam Practice Tip**

If you can't see how to find the angle you've been asked for, try finding other angles in the diagram first — chances are you'll be able to use them to find the one you need. You'll probably have to use a few of the angle rules to get to the answer — if you get stuck just try each rule until you get to one that you can use.

Score

22

Section Three — Geometry and Measure

# Parallel Lines

**1** *AB* and *CD* are parallel lines. *EF* is a straight line.

Work out the size of angles *x* and *y*, giving reasons for your answers.

........................................................................................

........................................................................................

........................................................................................

........................................................................................

*[Total 4 marks]*

*Diagram not drawn to scale*

**2** *BD* and *EF* are parallel straight lines. *AH* is a straight line.

Work out the value of *x*.

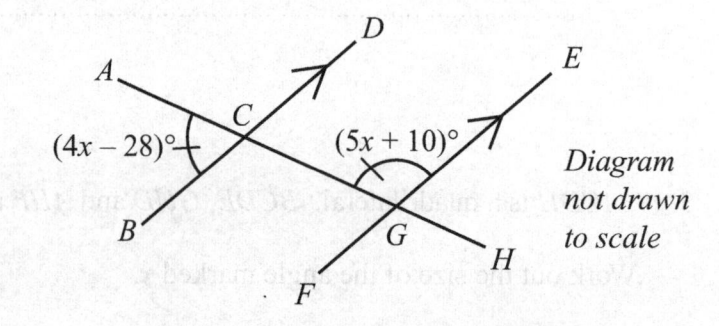

*Diagram not drawn to scale*

*x* = ........................

*[Total 3 marks]*

**3** *AGF* and *BD* are parallel lines. *AEDC* and *BEG* are straight lines.

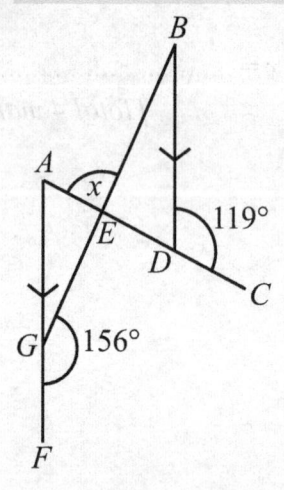

Work out the size of angle *x*.

*Marks will be awarded for the organisation, communication and written accuracy of your answer.*

*Diagram not drawn to scale*

*x* = ........................°

*[4 + 2 OCW]*

*[Total 6 marks]*

Score:

13

Section Three — Geometry and Measure

# Circle Geometry

1   ABCD is a cyclic quadrilateral. EAF is a tangent to the circle.
    AB passes through the centre of the circle, O.

   a)  Calculate the size of angle BAD,
       giving a reason for your answer.

       ....................................................................................................

       ....................................................................................................
                                                                          [2]

   b)  Hence, find the size of angle DAF.

                                                                    .......................°
                                                                          [2]
                                                                  [Total 4 marks]

   *Diagram not drawn to scale*

2   A, B, C and D are points on the circumference of a circle.
    Angle BCD is 28° and angle ADC is 24°.

   a)  Find the sizes of angles x and y.

       x = ....................°          y = ....................°
                                                                          [2]

   b)  Give a reason for your answers.

       ....................................................................................................

       ....................................................................................................
                                                                          [1]
                                                                  [Total 3 marks]

   *Diagram not drawn to scale*

3   B and C are points on the circumference of a circle with centre O.
    AB and AC are tangents to the circle.

   a)  State the length AB.

                                                         ..................... cm
                                                                          [1]

   b)  Calculate the size of angle AOC.

                                                         .....................°
                                                                          [2]

   *Diagram not drawn to scale*

   c)  Hence, find the size of angle BOC.

                                                         .....................°
                                                                          [1]
                                                                  [Total 4 marks]

Section Three — Geometry and Measure

**4** The diagram shows a circle, centre O. A, B, C and D are points on the circumference.

Work out the size of angle ADC. Give reasons for your working.

..................................................................................................................

..................................................................................................................

..................................................................................................................

..................................................................................................................

..................................................................................................................

*Diagram not drawn to scale*

[Total 4 marks]

**5** In the diagram, O is the centre of the circle. B, C and D are points on the circumference of the circle and AD and AB are tangents. Angle DAB is 80°.

Work out the size of angle BCD.

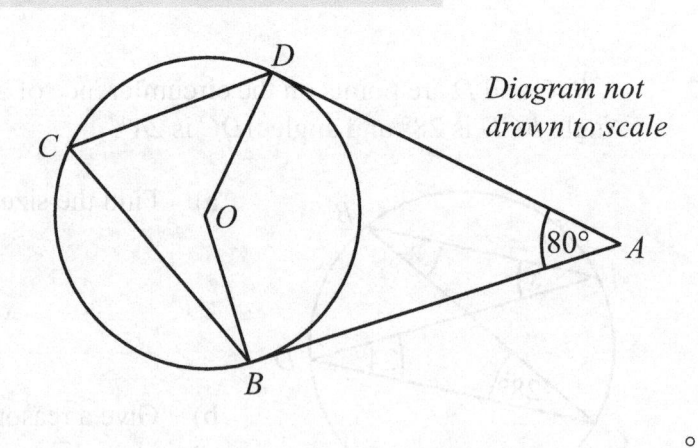

*Diagram not drawn to scale*

.......................... °

[Total 3 marks]

**6** The diagram below shows a circle with centre O. A, B, C and D are points on the circumference of the circle and AOC is a straight line.

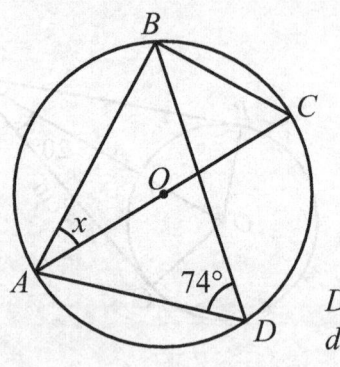

Work out the size of the angle marked x.

*Diagram not drawn to scale*

x = .......................... °

[Total 3 marks]

### Exam Practice Tip
Make sure you know the rules about circles really, really well. Draw them out and stick them all over your bedroom walls, your fridge, even your dog. Then in the exam, go through the rules one by one and use them to fill in as many angles in the diagram as you can. Keep an eye out for sneaky isosceles triangles too.

Score

21

Section Three — Geometry and Measure

# Loci and Construction

**1** *EFG* is an isosceles triangle. Sides *EG* and *FG* are both 4.5 cm long.

Side *EF* has been drawn here.

E ——————— F

a) Complete the construction of triangle *EFG* by drawing sides *EG* and *FG*.

[2]

b) Construct the bisector of angle *EGF*.

[2]

[Total 4 marks]

**2** *AB* is a straight line.

Use a ruler and a pair of compasses to construct the perpendicular bisector of the line *AB*. Show all of your construction lines.

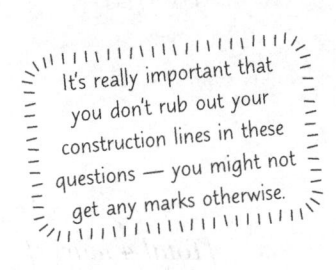

*It's really important that you don't rub out your construction lines in these questions — you might not get any marks otherwise.*

A ———
    ——— B

[Total 2 marks]

**3** *RST* is a straight line.

Use a ruler and a pair of compasses to construct an angle of 30° to the line *RST* at the point *S*. Show all of your construction lines.

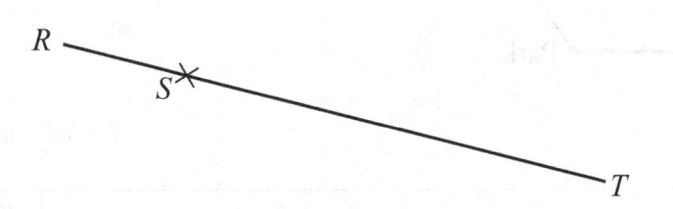

R ——— S× ———— T

[Total 4 marks]

Section Three — Geometry and Measure

**4** A kite *ABCD* has sides *AB* and *CB* of length 4 cm and sides *AD* and *CD* of length 7 cm. The shorter diagonal of the kite, *AC*, has a length of 3 cm.

Construct an accurate, full-size drawing of the kite and label the corners. Show all your construction lines.

C
|
|
A

*[Total 4 marks]*

**5** *ABC* is a triangle.

Find and shade the region inside the triangle which is **both** closer to the line *AB* than the line *BC*, **and** also more than 6.5 cm from the point *C*.

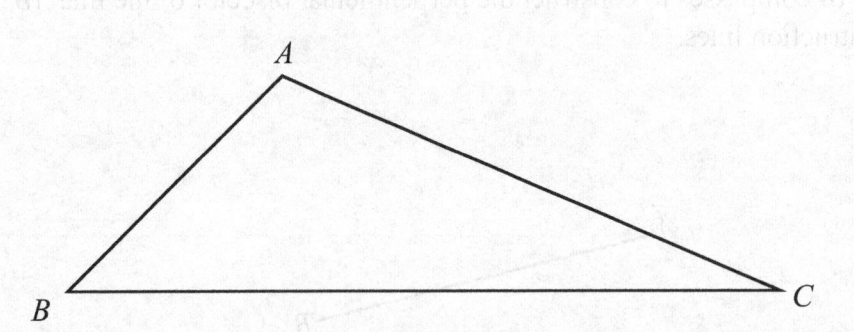

*Start by bisecting the angle ABC.*

*[Total 4 marks]*

**6** A council are putting up a new visitor information board. They want it to be within the area shown below, closer to the park than to the library, but also closer to the station than to the park.

Shade the region where the board could be placed.

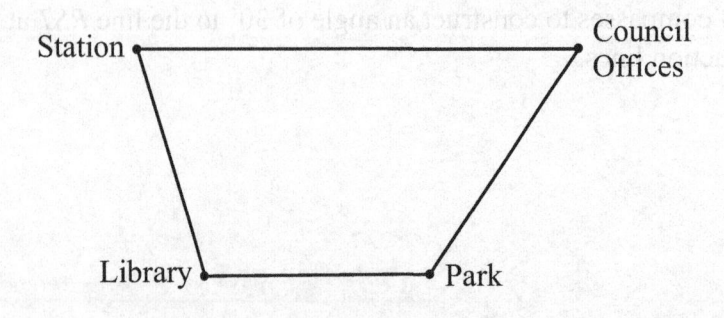

Station • — — — • Council Offices

Library • — — • Park

*[Total 4 marks]*

**Exam Practice Tip**
Always draw your construction lines as accurately as possible — make sure your compass is set to the correct length before you draw each arc. You can check the accuracy of your construction at the end by measuring the lengths of the sides with a ruler or the sizes of the angles with a protractor.

Score

22

Section Three — Geometry and Measure

# Bearings and Scale Drawings

**1** Douglas drew a scale drawing of one of the rooms in his house.

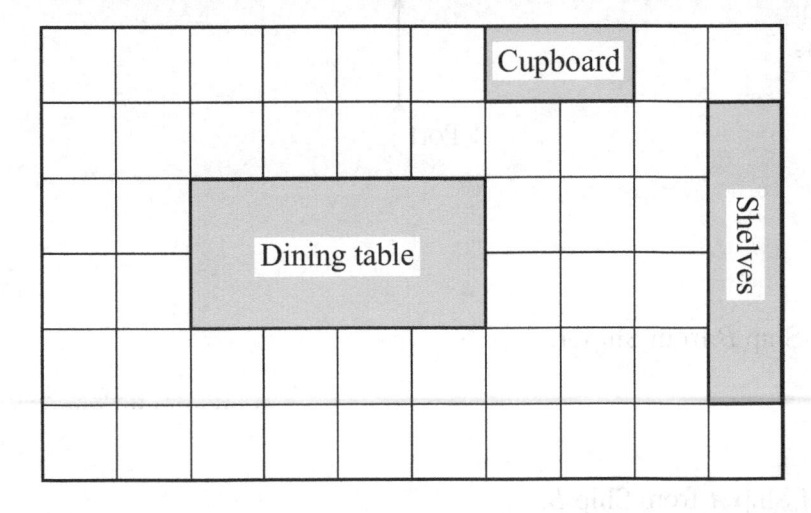

a) His dining table is 2 m long. What is the scale of this drawing?

1 cm represents .................... m
*[1]*

b) Work out the real distance from the dining table to the shelves.

.................... m
*[1]*

c) Douglas wants to put a chair measuring 1 m × 1.5 m in the room so that there is a space of at least 0.5 m around it. Is this possible? Give a reason for your answer.

..............................................................................................................................

..............................................................................................................................
*[2]*

*[Total 4 marks]*

**2** The instructions on a treasure map say "start at the cross and walk 400 metres on a bearing of 150°. Then walk 500 metres on a bearing of 090° to find the treasure."

Using a scale of 1 cm = 100 m, accurately draw the path that must be taken to find the treasure on the map below.

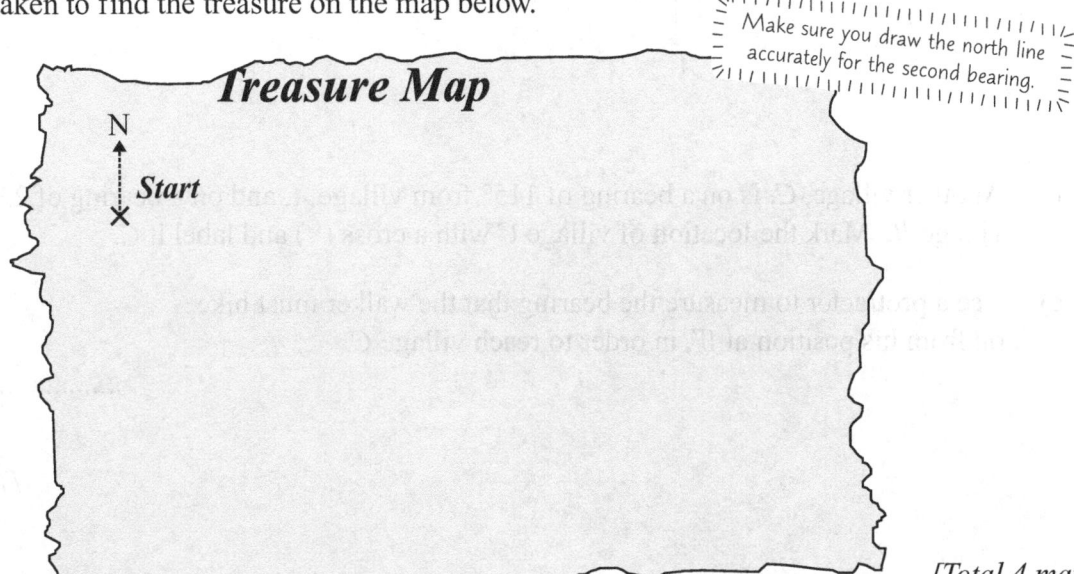

*Make sure you draw the north line accurately for the second bearing.*

*[Total 4 marks]*

Section Three — Geometry and Measure

**3** Two ships leave a port at the same time.
Ship *A* travels due west for 40 km. Ship *B* travels 30 km on a bearing of 110°.

a) Using a scale of 1 cm = 10 km,
draw the journeys of the two
ships in the space on the right
and mark their final positions.

N

Port

[4]

b) Measure the final bearing of Ship *B* from Ship *A*.

.................................°

[1]

c) Calculate the final bearing of Ship *A* from Ship *B*.

.................................°

[2]

[Total 7 marks]

**4** The diagram shows the position of two villages, *A* and *B*.

a) A walker hikes from village *A* on a bearing of 035°.
After an hour's walk he stops when village *B* is directly east of his position.
Mark the walker's position on the diagram with a cross (×) and label it *W*.

N

B

N

A

[2]

b) Another village, *C*, is on a bearing of 115° from village *A*, and on a bearing of 235° from village *B*. Mark the location of village *C* with a cross (×) and label it *C*.

[3]

c) Use a protractor to measure the bearing that the walker must hike on from his position at *W*, in order to reach village *C*.

.................................°

[1]

[Total 6 marks]

Score:

21

Section Three — Geometry and Measure

# Pythagoras' Theorem

**1** The diagram shows a right-angled triangle *ABC*.
*AC* is 4 cm long. *BC* is 8 cm long.

Calculate the length of *AB*.
Give your answer correct to 2 decimal places.

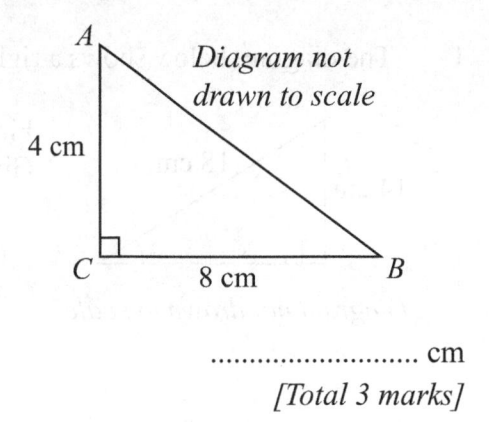

*Diagram not drawn to scale*

4 cm, 8 cm

.......................... cm
*[Total 3 marks]*

**2** Point *A* has coordinates (2, –1). Point *B* has coordinates (8, 8).
Find the length of the line segment *AB*. Give your answer correct to 3 significant figures.

..........................
*[Total 3 marks]*

**3** A triangle has a base of 10 cm. Its other two sides are both 13 cm long.

Calculate the area of the triangle.

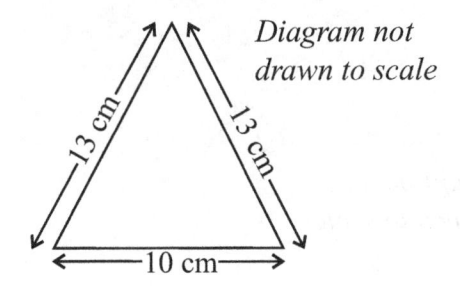

*Diagram not drawn to scale*

13 cm, 13 cm, 10 cm

*Start by finding the height of the triangle.*

.......................... cm²
*[Total 4 marks]*

**4** The diagram shows a kite *ABCD*. *AB* is 28.3 cm long.
*BC* is 54.3 cm long. *BE* is 20 cm in length.

Work out the perimeter of triangle *ABC*. Give your answer to correct 1 decimal place.

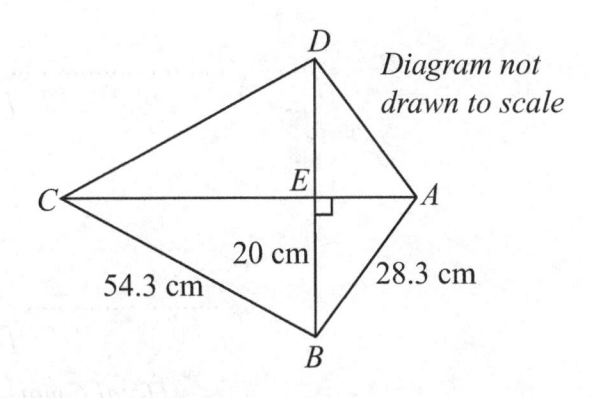

*Diagram not drawn to scale*

54.3 cm, 20 cm, 28.3 cm

.......................... cm
*[Total 5 marks]*

Score: 15

Section Three — Geometry and Measure

# Trigonometry — Sin, Cos, Tan

**1** The diagram below shows a right-angled triangle.

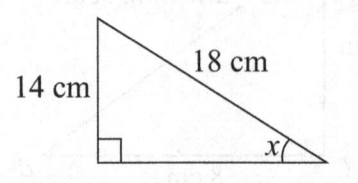

Find the size of the angle marked $x$.
Give your answer correct to 1 decimal place.

14 cm, 18 cm, $x$

*Diagram not drawn to scale*

.......................... °

*[Total 3 marks]*

**2** The diagram on the right shows a right-angled triangle.

Find the length of the side marked $y$.
Give your answer correct to 3 significant figures.

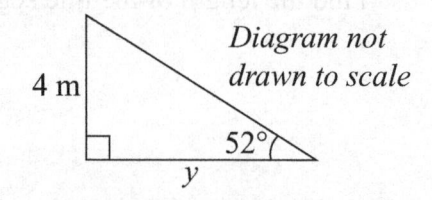

4 m, 52°, $y$

*Diagram not drawn to scale*

.......................... m

*[Total 3 marks]*

**3** In the triangle below, $AB = BC = 10$ m and angle $C = 34°$.

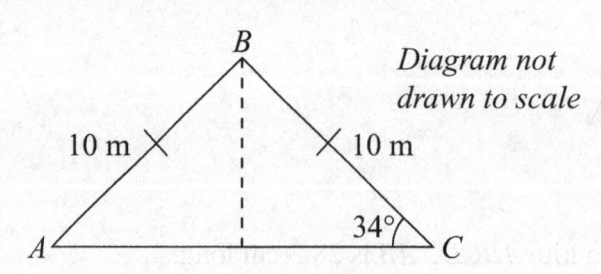

*Diagram not drawn to scale*

10 m, 10 m, 34°, A, B, C

a) Calculate the height of the triangle.
   Give your answer correct to 2 decimal places.

.......................... m
*[3]*

b) Calculate the length $AC$.
   Give your answer correct to 2 decimal places.

.......................... m
*[3]*

*[Total 6 marks]*

Section Three — Geometry and Measure

**4** A shopkeeper needs a new access ramp for his shop.
The top of the ramp must be level with the top of the step, which is 12 cm high.
The start of the ramp is 191 cm from the step.

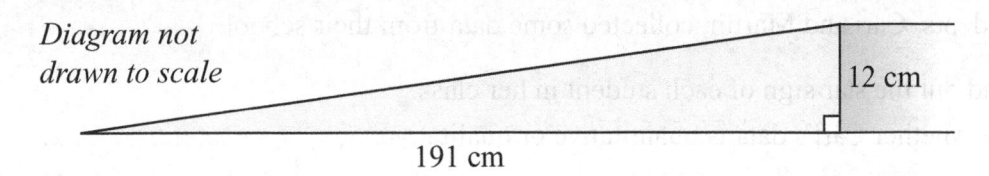

*Diagram not drawn to scale*

12 cm

191 cm

Calculate the angle of depression of the start of the ramp from the top of the step.
Give your answer correct to 1 decimal place.

.......................... °
[Total 3 marks]

**5** A helicopter takes off from point *H* and travels for 20 miles on a bearing of 254°.
It then turns sharply and travels due north.

For how many miles would the helicopter need to travel in this direction before
it is due west of point *H*? Give your answer correct to 2 significant figures.

*Sketching a diagram might help you here.*

.......................... miles
[Total 4 marks]

**6** *X*, *Y* and *Z* are points on a circle, where *XY* is a diameter of the circle.

*Diagram not drawn to scale*

58°

4 cm

35°

Calculate the length of *YZ*, giving your answer correct to 2 decimal places.

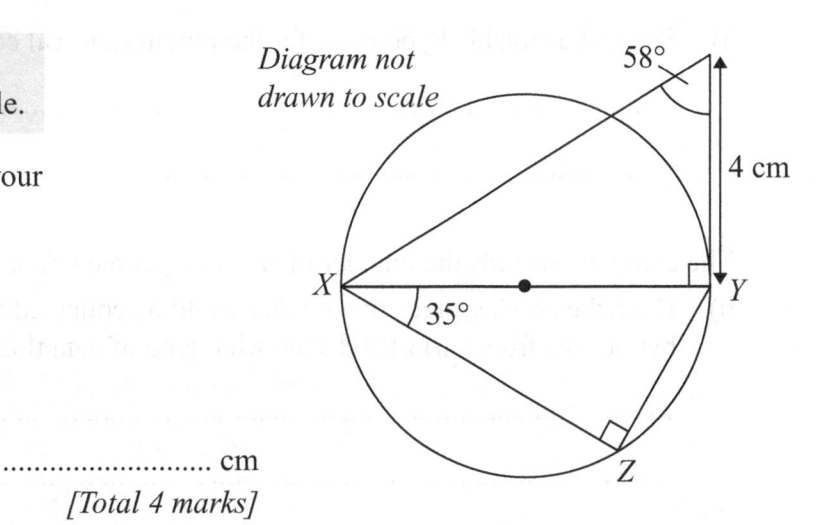

.......................... cm
[Total 4 marks]

**Exam Practice Tip**
In an exam, it'll help if you start by labelling the sides of a right-angled triangle, opposite (O), adjacent (A) and hypotenuse (H) — these are easy to get muddled up. If you're working out an angle, make sure you check whether it's sensible — if you get an angle of 720° or 0.0072° it's probably wrong, so give it another go.

**Score**

23

Section Three — Geometry and Measure

# Section Four — Statistics

# Planning an Investigation

**1** Two students, Cari and Martin, collected some data from their school.

Cari found out the star sign of each student in her class.

a) State whether Cari's data is quantitative or qualitative. ...................................

[1]

Martin found out the number of students late to school one day.
His data is quantitative.

b) State whether Martin's data is discrete or continuous. ...................................

[1]

[Total 2 marks]

**2** A music shop sells CDs, DVDs, tapes and vinyl records.

a) Suggest one example of qualitative data that could be collected by the shop.

................................................................................................................................

................................................................................................................................

[1]

b) Suggest one example of quantitative data that could be collected by the shop.

................................................................................................................................

................................................................................................................................

[1]

[Total 2 marks]

**3** A pharmaceutical company wants to investigate whether their new product is a better acne treatment than their previous product.

a) Suggest a suitable hypothesis for the pharmaceutical company to test.

................................................................................................................................

................................................................................................................................

[1]

The company records the number of spots on people's faces before using the treatment.

b) Describe another piece of data that could be collected to test the hypothesis from part a) and state what type of data this is.

................................................................................................................................

................................................................................................................................

[2]

[Total 3 marks]

Score: 7

# Sampling and Collecting Data

**1** A scientist is researching the lifespan of deer in Snowdonia.
She takes a sample of 100 deer from different locations in Snowdonia.

a) Identify the population used by the scientist.

...................................................................................................................................................

*[1]*

b) Suggest one reason why it's sensible for the scientist to take a sample.

...................................................................................................................................................

*[1]*

*[Total 2 marks]*


**2** Geraint is investigating the incomes of people in a town.
He uses the telephone book to choose a sample of people from the town.

a) Give one reason why this might not be an appropriate sample to use.

...................................................................................................................................................

...................................................................................................................................................

*[1]*

Geraint uses a sample of 10 people to investigate the incomes of people in the town.

b) Suggest one way that he could make the results of his investigation more reliable.

...................................................................................................................................................

...................................................................................................................................................

*[1]*

*[Total 2 marks]*


**3** Fflur wants to find out how often teenagers buy chocolate bars.

She writes the following question to ask in a survey.

| How many chocolate bars have you bought? |
| 1 – 2    2 – 3    3 – 4 |
| ☐         ☐         ☐   |

Write down two things that are wrong with the question above.

1 ................................................................................................................................................

2 ................................................................................................................................................

*[Total 2 marks]*

Section Four — Statistics

**4** Circle either true or false for each of the statements in the table.

| Products on a conveyor belt are being quality assessed. A systematic sample of the products is taken. It's possible for the sample to consist of the 3rd, 7th, 11th and 16th products. | true | false |
|---|---|---|
| Half of all the people in a random sample say that they watch television every day. This means that half of all the people in the population watch television every day. | true | false |
| The masses, $m$ kg, of several bags of sand are measured and the results grouped into these classes: $0 < m < 3$, $3 \leq m < 6$, $6 \leq m < 9$, $9 \leq m$. These classes cover all possible masses. | true | false |

*[Total 2 marks]*

**5** A company that makes springs wants to find out if springs from a batch of 5000 are faulty.

Describe how the company could use systematic sampling to check 100 springs from the batch.

................................................................................................................................................................

................................................................................................................................................................

................................................................................................................................................................

*[Total 3 marks]*

**6** Waqar asked 50 people at a football match how they travelled there. He found that 22 of them travelled by car. There were 5000 people at the match altogether.

a) Use the information above to estimate the number of people who travelled to the match by car.

..............

*[3]*

b) Daisy was at a different football match on the same day. She uses Waqar's sample data to estimate that 374 of the 850 people at her match travelled there by car.

Explain the assumption Daisy has made and comment on the reliability of her estimate.

................................................................................................................................................................

................................................................................................................................................................

................................................................................................................................................................

*[2]*

> Remember: to get reliable estimates, a sample needs to fairly represent the population.

*[Total 5 marks]*

Score: ☐

**16**

Section Four — Statistics

# Mean, Median, Mode and Range

**1** Cath has baked 24 Welshcakes. The mean diameter of the Welshcakes is 6 cm.

Circle either true or false for each of the statements in the table.

| The median diameter of the Welshcakes must also be 6 cm. | true | false |
| --- | --- | --- |
| If there are some Welshcakes bigger than 6 cm, there must also be some smaller than 6 cm. | true | false |
| At least one of the Welshcakes must have a diameter of exactly 6 cm. | true | false |
| There must be the same number of Welshcakes that are larger than 6 cm and smaller than 6 cm. | true | false |
| The range of diameters of the Welshcakes must be less than 6 cm. | true | false |

*[Total 2 marks]*

**2** Danny thinks of three different whole numbers that have a range of 6 and a mean of 4.

Write down three possible numbers he could be thinking of.

.................., .................., ..................

*[Total 2 marks]*

**3** The mean of twelve numbers is 5 and the mode is 7. Ten of the numbers are shown in the table.

| 1 | 5 | 7 | 2 | 3 | .............. |
| --- | --- | --- | --- | --- | --- |
| 6 | 7 | 9 | 8 | 2 | .............. |

a) Given that the numbers are non-zero and positive, fill in the two missing numbers.

*[3]*

b) An extra number 6 is added, so that there are now thirteen numbers in total. Describe the effect that this would have on the mean.

.......................................................................................................................

*[1]*

*[Total 4 marks]*

**Exam Practice Tip**

It's key that you know what the mean, median, mode and range actually are and how you calculate them. Exam questions might test your understanding of averages by stating them and asking you to find the original numbers or asking you what effect an extra number could have on the mean or median.

Score: 8

Section Four — Statistics

# Averages and Spread

**1** A manufacturer tested the lifetimes (to the nearest 10 hours) of a type of LED light bulb so that he could confidently say how long they lasted. The results for eight such light bulbs are as follows:

| 3090 | 2010 | 2030 | 2750 | 90 | 2620 | 2800 | 2550 |

a) A customer asks the manufacturer how long, on average, this type of LED light bulb lasts.

(i) Explain why the median would be a more appropriate average to use than the mean.

....................................................................................................................................

....................................................................................................................................
[1]

(ii) Calculate the median lifetime of the bulbs.

*Make sure your answer refers to the context of the question.*

.............. hours
[2]

b) The median lifetime of another type of bulb is 1975 hours. Compare the lifetimes of the two types of light bulb.

....................................................................................................................................

....................................................................................................................................
[1]

[Total 4 marks]

**2** The data below shows the number of strawberries collected from each plant during the harvest of two strawberry patches.

Patch A:    8    13    19    22    8    18    14    16    9    14    12
Patch B:    14    19    11    13    15    11    13

a) For each patch, work out the interquartile range for the number of strawberries harvested.

*To calculate the interquartile range, you'll first want to put the data in order and then think about the quartiles.*

Patch A: ..............     Patch B: ..............
[4]

b) Using your results from part a), give one comparison between the plants in Patch A and the plants in Patch B.

....................................................................................................................................

....................................................................................................................................
[1]

[Total 5 marks]

Score:    9

Section Four — Statistics

# Simple Charts and Graphs

**1** The numbers of swallows seen in Dylan's garden over a year are shown in the graph below.

Dylan uses the graph to suggest that there were 12 swallows in his garden in August. Do you agree with this?
Give a reason for your answer.

..................................................................................................

..................................................................................................

..................................................................................................

..................................................................................................

*[Total 1 mark]*

**2** A cafe sells tea and coffee. The numbers of teas and coffees sold one week are shown in this dual bar chart.

a) What percentage of the drinks sold on Wednesday were tea?
Give your answer correct to 1 decimal place.

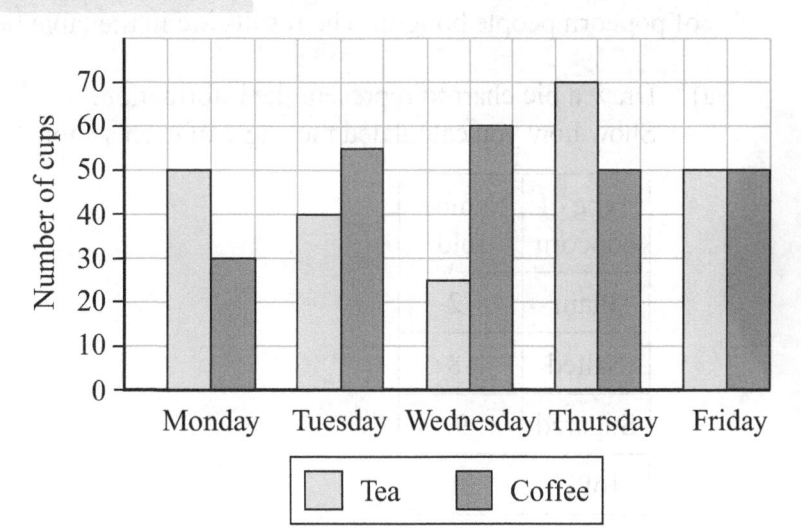

.................. %
*[2]*

b) (i) Find the range of the numbers of coffees sold.

..........................................
*[2]*

(ii) Find the mean number of total drinks sold per day.

..........................................
*[3]*

*[Total 7 marks]*

Score:

8

Section Four — Statistics

# Pie Charts

**1** A survey was carried out at a leisure centre to find out which sport people prefer to do. The results are shown in the pie chart.

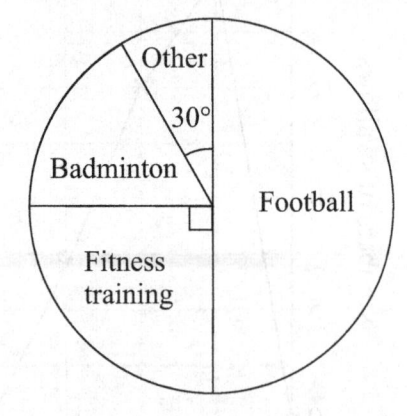

a) What fraction of people prefer to do fitness training?

........................
[1]

60 people said they prefer to play football.

b) How many people prefer to play badminton?

........................
[2]

[Total 3 marks]

**2** A survey was carried out in a local cinema to find out which flavour of popcorn people bought. The results are in the table below.

a) Draw a pie chart to represent the information.
Show how you calculated the angle of each sector.

| Type of popcorn | Number sold |
|---|---|
| Plain | 12 |
| Salted | 18 |
| Sugared | 9 |
| Toffee | 21 |

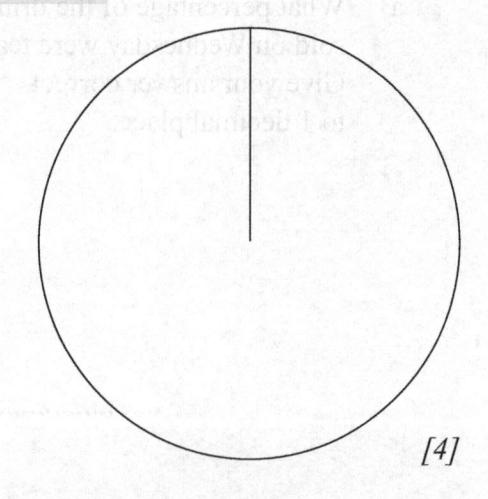

[4]

Another survey was carried out to find out which flavour of ice cream people bought. The results are shown in the pie chart below. Gavin compares the two pie charts and says:

"The results show that more people bought strawberry ice cream than toffee popcorn."

b) Explain whether or not Gavin is right.

................................................................................................

................................................................................................

................................................................................................

[1]

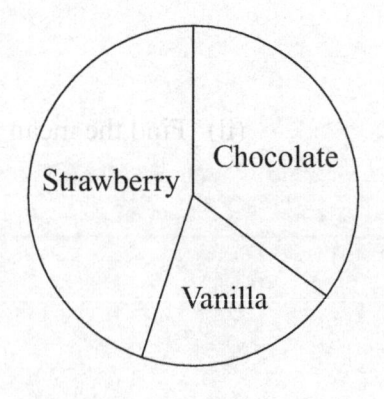

[Total 5 marks]

Section Four — Statistics

# Scatter Diagrams

**1** 15 pupils in a class study both Spanish and Italian.
Their end of year exam results are shown on the scatter diagram below.

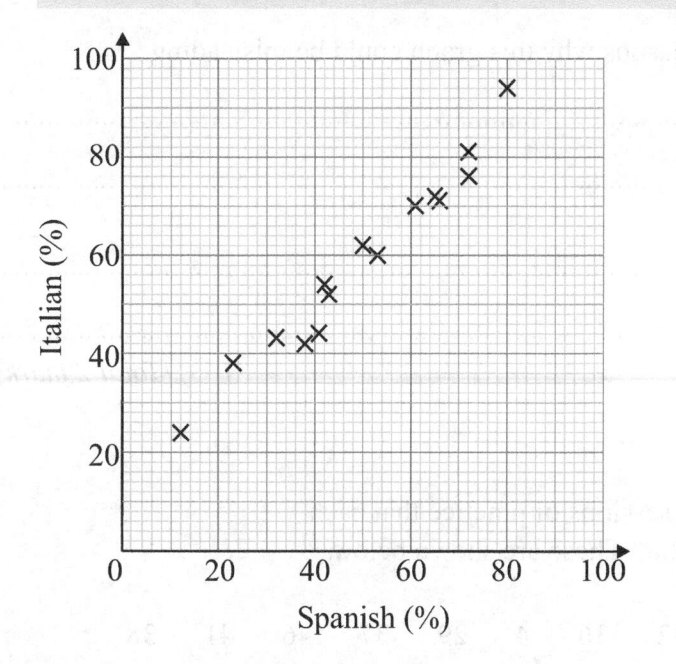

a) Give the type of correlation shown on the graph.

...................................................................
*[1]*

b) By eye, draw a line of best fit for the data.
*[1]*

c) Ahmed was absent for his Spanish exam but scored 66% on his Italian exam. Estimate the mark he might have got in Spanish.

.........................
*[1]*

*[Total 3 marks]*

**2** A furniture company is looking at how effective their advertising is.
They are comparing how much they spent on advertising in random months with their total sales value for that month. This information is shown on the diagram below.

The table shows the amount spent on advertising and the value of sales for three more months.

| Amount spent on advertising (thousands of pounds) | 0.75 | 0.15 | 1.85 |
|---|---|---|---|
| Sales (thousands of pounds) | 105 | 60 | 170 |

a) Plot the information from the table on the scatter diagram.
*[1]*

b) Rees says, "The diagram shows that if we increase our spending on advertising, we'll see an increase in sales." Explain whether or not you agree with his statement.

..............................................................
..............................................................
..............................................................
*[1]*

*[Total 2 marks]*

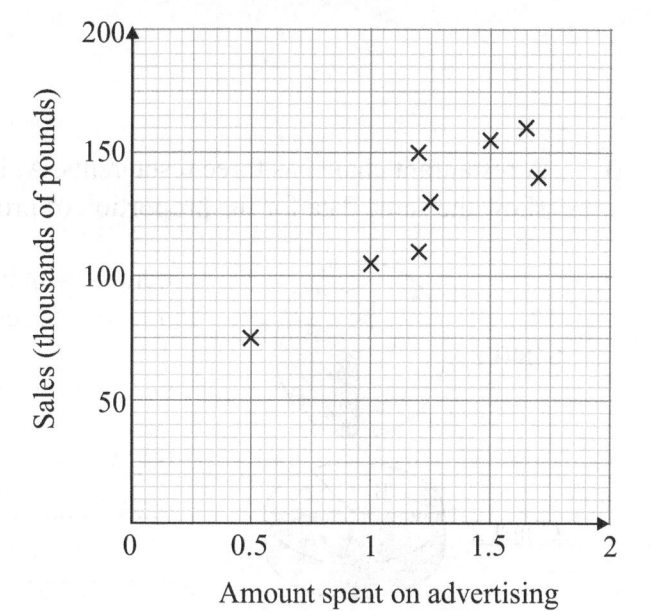

Score: 5

Section Four — Statistics

# Interpreting Data

**1** A report on the levels of pollution caused by vehicles contains the graph below, which shows the number of flights per day from a particular airport over time.

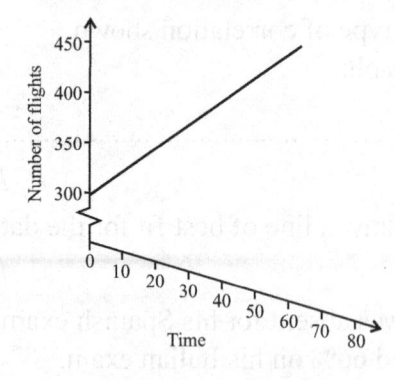

Give **two** reasons why this graph could be misleading.

1) ......................................................................
......................................................................

2) ......................................................................
......................................................................

*[Total 2 marks]*

**2** A rugby club coach records the number of sessions of practice that each of the members of the club attended one year. These are shown below.

31  43  48  41  49  32  36  4  29  37  46  41  38

Would the range or the interquartile range be more useful in analysing this data?
Explain your answer.

......................................................................
......................................................................

*[Total 2 marks]*

**3** A restaurant chain has three restaurants, A, B and C. The pie charts below show the same data for the proportion of profit by each of the restaurants.

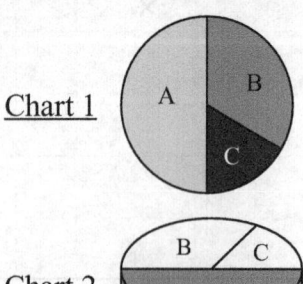

Chart 1

Chart 2

Chart 3

Identify which one of the diagrams is misleading in favour of restaurant A and explain why.

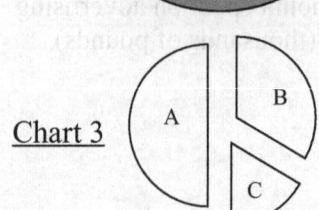

......................................................................
......................................................................
......................................................................
......................................................................

*[Total 2 marks]*

Score: 6

Section Four — Statistics

# Frequency Tables — Finding Averages

**1** The table on the right shows the number of pets owned by each pupil in a school class.

| Number of pets | Frequency |
|---|---|
| 0 | 8 |
| 1 | 3 |
| 2 | 5 |
| 3 | 8 |
| 4 | 4 |
| 5 | 1 |
| 6 | 0 |

    a) What is the range of this data?

.....................
*[1]*

    b) Work out the mean number of pets per pupil.

*Add an extra column to the table to help you.*

.....................
*[4]*

    c) Find the median number of pets.

.....................
*[2]*

*[Total 7 marks]*

**2** A quality control department checked the number of nails in 180 bags, each of which should contain 100 nails. The numbers of nails that they found in the bags are shown in the table below.

| Number of nails per bag | 97 | 98 | 99 | 100 | 101 |
|---|---|---|---|---|---|
| Number of bags | 6 | 20 | 44 | 108 | 2 |

    a) What is the modal number of nails in a bag?

.....................
*[1]*

    b) What is the median number of nails in a bag?

.....................
*[2]*

    c) Calculate the mean number of nails in a bag. Give your answer correct to 1 decimal place.

.....................
*[4]*

*[Total 7 marks]*

Score: ☐ / 14

Section Four — Statistics

# Grouped Frequency Tables

1   For a science experiment, Bill planted 10 seeds and measured their growth to the nearest cm after 12 days. His results are shown in the table below.

| Growth in cm | Number of plants |
|---|---|
| $0 \leq x \leq 2$ | 2 |
| $3 \leq x \leq 5$ | 4 |
| $6 \leq x \leq 8$ | 3 |
| $9 \leq x \leq 11$ | 1 |

a) Find the modal class.

...........................
*[1]*

b) Find the class which contains the median.

...........................
*[1]*

c) Bill works out that the mean height after 12 days is 12 cm.
Explain why Bill must have made a mistake.

................................................................................................................
*[1]*
*[Total 3 marks]*

2   The table shows the times it took 32 pupils at a school to run a 200 m sprint.

a) Calculate an estimate for the mean time taken.

| Time ($t$ seconds) | Frequency | Mid-interval value | Frequency × Mid-interval value |
|---|---|---|---|
| $22 < t \leq 26$ | 4 | $(22 + 26) \div 2 = 24$ | $4 \times 24 =$ ............ |
| $26 < t \leq 30$ | 8 | | |
| $30 < t \leq 34$ | 13 | | |
| $34 < t \leq 38$ | 6 | | |
| $38 < t \leq 42$ | 1 | | |
| Total | | | |

Estimate of mean = ..................... ÷ ..................... = .....................

..................... seconds
*[4]*

All pupils with a time of 34 seconds or less qualified for the next round.

b) Musashi says that fewer than 20% of the pupils failed to qualify for the next round.
Comment on Musashi's statement and show working to support your answer.

................................................................................................................

................................................................................................................
*[2]*
*[Total 6 marks]*

Score:

9

Section Four — Statistics

# Frequency Polygons and Diagrams

**1** Cerys records the heights (x cm) of players on two school football teams in the table below.

| Height (x cm) | 150 ≤ x < 160 | 160 ≤ x < 170 | 170 ≤ x < 180 | 180 ≤ x < 190 | 190 ≤ x < 200 |
|---|---|---|---|---|---|
| Team A | 0 | 1 | 2 | 7 | 1 |
| Team B | 1 | 4 | 5 | 1 | 0 |

Cerys shows her results for Team A on the frequency polygon below.

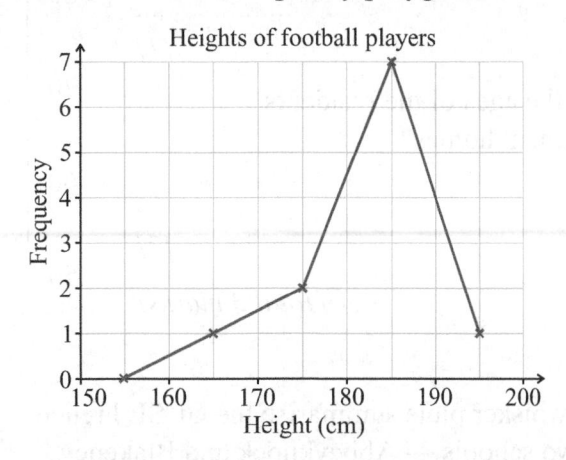

a) Complete the graph by showing the results for Team B on the same set of axes.

*[2]*

b) Cerys says that the players on Team A are generally taller than those on Team B.
Explain how the frequency polygon supports this view.

..................................................................................................................................................

..................................................................................................................................................

*[1]*

*[Total 3 marks]*

**2** The grouped frequency diagram below shows the average speed (s km/h) of 200 cyclists in a race.

25 cyclists had an average speed of 30 < s ≤ 35 km/h.
Use the diagram to complete the table.

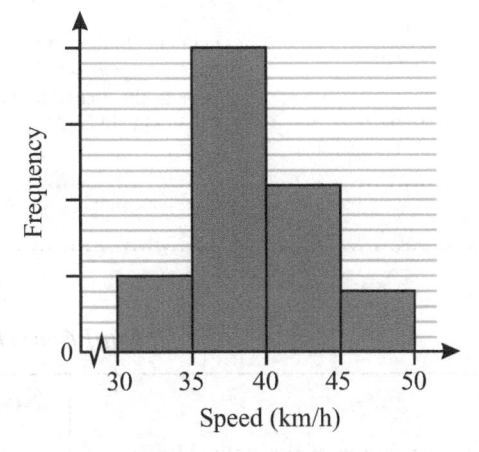

| Speed (s km/h) | Frequency |
|---|---|
| 30 < s ≤ 35 | 25 |
| 35 < s ≤ 40 | ................ |
| 40 < s ≤ 45 | ................ |
| 45 < s ≤ 50 | ................ |

*[Total 2 marks]*

Score: ☐ / 5

Section Four — Statistics

# Box-and-Whisker Plots

**1** The box-and-whisker plots on the right show the ages of the residents in three retirement homes (A, B and C).

a) Which retirement home had the youngest residents on average?

.................... 
[1]

b) What is the range of the ages of the residents across all three retirement homes?

.................... 
[2]

[Total 3 marks]

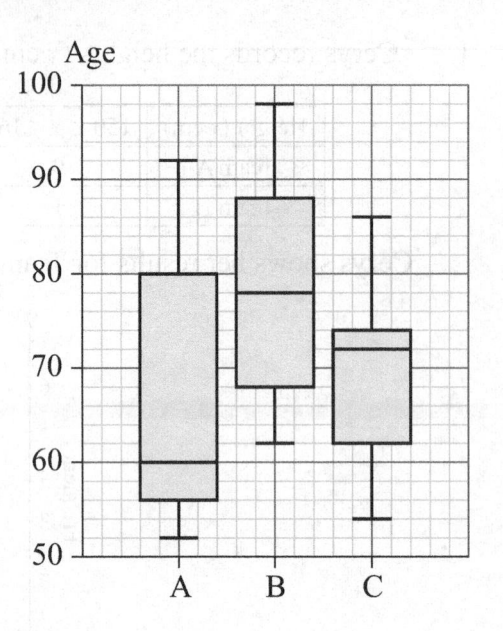

**2** The following box-and-whisker plots summarise the GCSE French results for students of two schools — Abbeyknock and Blakeney.

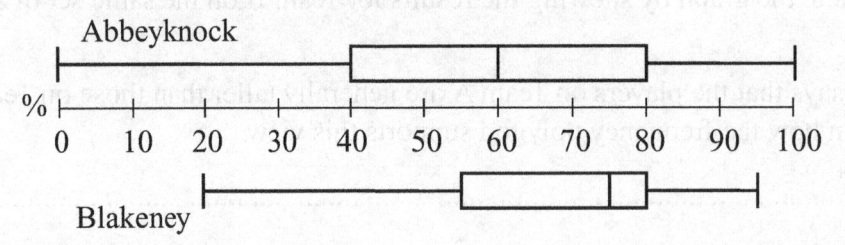

a) Use the box-and-whisker plot to identify the median result for the students of Abbeyknock.

.................... %
[1]

b) Calculate the interquartile range of the results for the students of Blakeney.

.................... %
[2]

c) Compare the two schools' results in relation to the medians and interquartile ranges.

*Make sure your comparisons refer to the French results.*

....................................................................................................................

....................................................................................................................

....................................................................................................................

....................................................................................................................

[3]

[Total 6 marks]

### Exam Practice Tip
When comparing two box-and-whisker plots, remember that the median is an average of the data, whereas the range and interquartile range are measures of spread (which show how consistent the data values are). Don't get confused if the plot is in an unusual orientation — all the values are found in just the same way.

Score: 9

Section Four — Statistics

# Cumulative Frequency

**1** 120 pupils in a year group sit an examination at the end of the year. Their results are given in the table below.

| Exam mark (%) | $0 < x \leq 20$ | $20 < x \leq 30$ | $30 < x \leq 40$ | $40 < x \leq 50$ | $50 < x \leq 60$ | $60 < x \leq 70$ | $70 < x \leq 80$ | $80 < x \leq 100$ |
|---|---|---|---|---|---|---|---|---|
| Frequency | 3 | 10 | 12 | 24 | 42 | 16 | 9 | 4 |

a) Complete this cumulative frequency table:

| Exam mark (%) | ≤ 20 | ≤ 30 | ≤ 40 | ≤ 50 | ≤ 60 | ≤ 70 | ≤ 80 | ≤ 100 |
|---|---|---|---|---|---|---|---|---|
| Cumulative Frequency | 3 | 13 | ...... | ...... | ...... | ...... | ...... | 120 |

*[1]*

b) Use your table to draw a cumulative frequency diagram on the axes below.

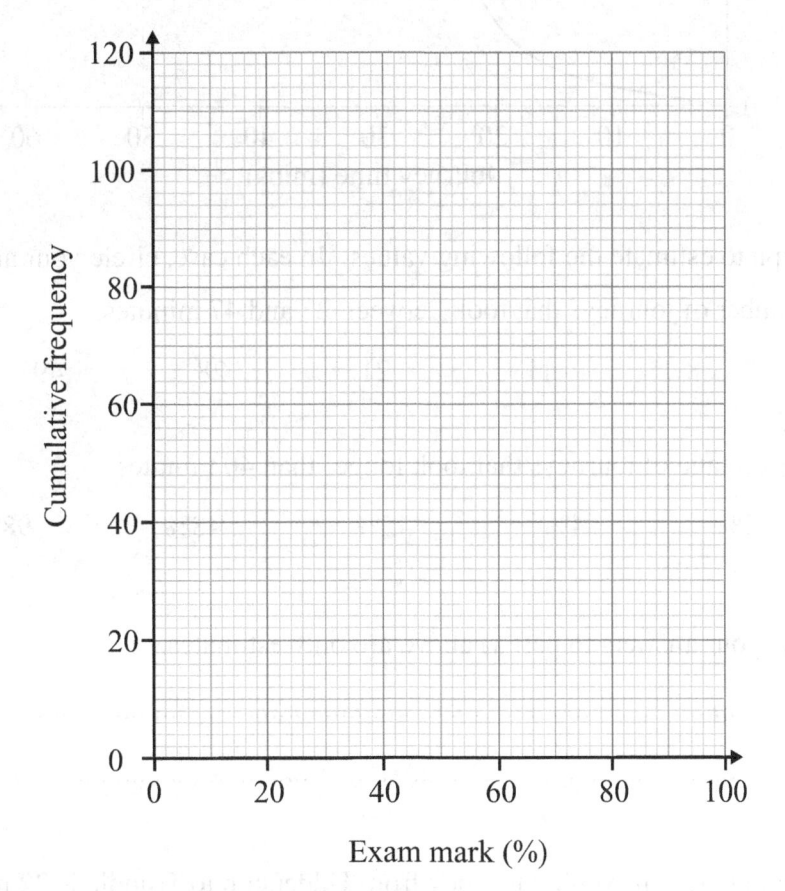

*[2]*

c) Use your diagram to find an estimate for the median mark.

................ %
*[1]*

d) Use your diagram to find an estimate for the interquartile range.

................ %
*[2]*

*[Total 6 marks]*

Section Four — Statistics

**2** The cumulative frequency graph below gives information about the length of time it takes to travel between Udderston and Trundle each morning. The graph has been drawn using the data from a grouped frequency table.

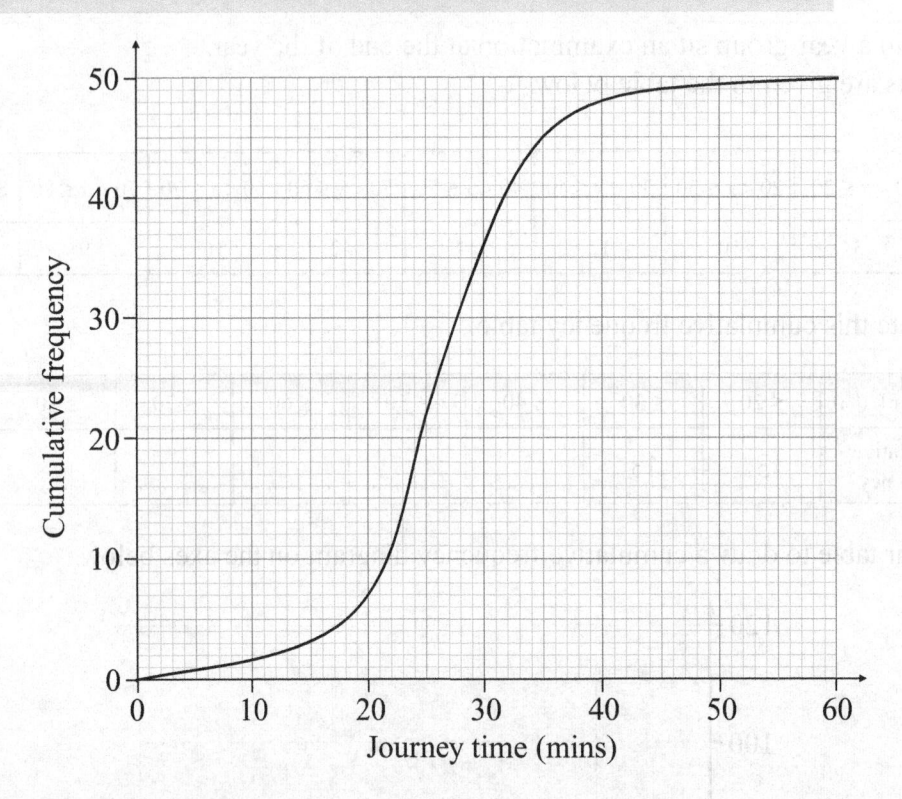

a) Use the graph to estimate the following values. In each case, circle your answer.

   i) The number of journeys that took between 27 and 47 minutes.

           8          11          21          28          49

   *[1]*

   ii) The percentage of journeys that took longer than 40 minutes.

           2%          4%          45%          48%          98%

   *[1]*

b) Explain why your answers to part a) above are only estimates.

   ..................................................................................................................................

   ..................................................................................................................................

   *[1]*

c) The median time for an evening journey from Udderston to Trundle is 22 minutes.
   Give one comparison of the morning and evening journey times from Udderston to Trundle.

   ..................................................................................................................................

   ..................................................................................................................................

   *[2]*

   *[Total 5 marks]*

Score:

**11**

Section Four — Statistics

# Probability Basics

**1** On the probability scale below, mark with a cross the probabilities of events a)-c).

Make sure you label each event.

```
|-------------------|-------------------|
0                  0.5                  1
```

a) Rolling an odd number on a fair, six-sided dice.

*[1]*

b) Rolling a number less than 7 on a fair, six-sided dice.

*[1]*

c) **Not** rolling a 4 on a fair, six-sided dice.

*[1]*

*[Total 3 marks]*

**2** The pupils in a year group are divided into four forms: A, B, C and D.

| Form | A | B | C | D |
|---|---|---|---|---|
| Probability | 0.3 | 0.2 | 0.15 | ............. |

Complete the table above to find the probability that a student chosen at random is in form D.

*[Total 2 marks]*

**3** Bronwen has a bag containing strawberry and banana sweets in the ratio 2:5. She picks a sweet at random from the bag.

a) What is the probability that she picks a strawberry sweet from the bag?

........................

*[1]*

b) Bronwen says, "I am exactly twice as likely to pick a banana sweet as a strawberry sweet". Is Bronwen correct? Explain your answer.

..................................................................................................................

..................................................................................................................

*[2]*

*[Total 3 marks]*

Score: 

**8**

Section Four — Statistics

# Counting Outcomes

**1** Sara decides to attend two new after-school activities. She can do one on Monday and one on Thursday. Below are lists of the activities she could do on these days.

**Monday:** Hockey  Orchestra  Drama     **Thursday:** Netball  Choir  Orienteering

a) List all the possible combinations of two activities that Sara could do each week.

[2]

b) If Sara were to choose two activities at random, what would be the probability that she does at least one of hockey or choir?

.......................
[2]

[Total 4 marks]

**2** A shop sells three different meal deals. The possible meal deal options are:
• sandwich and drink    • sandwich and snack    • sandwich, snack and drink

There are 5 different sandwiches, 8 different drinks and 4 different snacks.
How many possible meal deal combinations are there?

Combinations of sandwich and drink = .............. × .............. = ..............

Combinations of sandwich and snack = .............. × .............. = ..............

Combinations of sandwich, snack and drink = .............. × .............. × .............. = ..............

Total number of possible combinations = .............. + .............. + .............. = ..............

.......................
[Total 3 marks]

**3** Saffir spins 5 fair spinners, each numbered 1-4. She writes down, in order, the number that each spinner lands on to generate a 5-digit number.

a) How many different possibilities are there for the 5-digit number she generates?

.......................
[1]

b) What is the probability of Saffir generating a 5-digit number not containing a 1?

.......................
[2]

[Total 3 marks]

**Exam Practice Tip**
When listing all the possible outcomes, it can be easy to make mistakes — so try to go through them in a sensible way. When each outcome is equally likely, you can find the probability of something by counting how many outcomes fit what you're being asked and dividing that by the total number of outcomes.

10

# Relative Frequency

**1** Suda has a 6-sided dice. The sides are numbered 1 to 6.
Suda rolls the dice 50 times. Her results are shown in the table below.

| Number | 1 | 2 | 3 | 4 | 5 | 6 |
|---|---|---|---|---|---|---|
| Frequency | 16 | 6 | 12 | 7 | 3 | 6 |
| Relative frequency | .......... | .......... | .......... | .......... | .......... | .......... |

a) Complete the table above.

[2]

b) Suda says, "The dice has 6 sides so the probability of it landing on a 1 is $\frac{1}{6}$."
Criticise Suda's statement.

............................................................................................................................

............................................................................................................................

[2]

c) She rolls the dice another 50 times. Should she expect the same results? Explain your answer.

............................................................................................................................

............................................................................................................................

[1]

*[Total 5 marks]*

**2** A coin is tossed several times.

| Number of tosses | 200 | 400 | 800 | 1600 |
|---|---|---|---|---|
| Number of tails | 76 | 164 | 304 | 416 |
| Relative frequency of tails | 0.38 | 0.41 | 0.38 | 0.26 |

The table on the right summarises the number of times the coin landed on tails.

a) Draw a relative frequency diagram on the axes below to show this information.

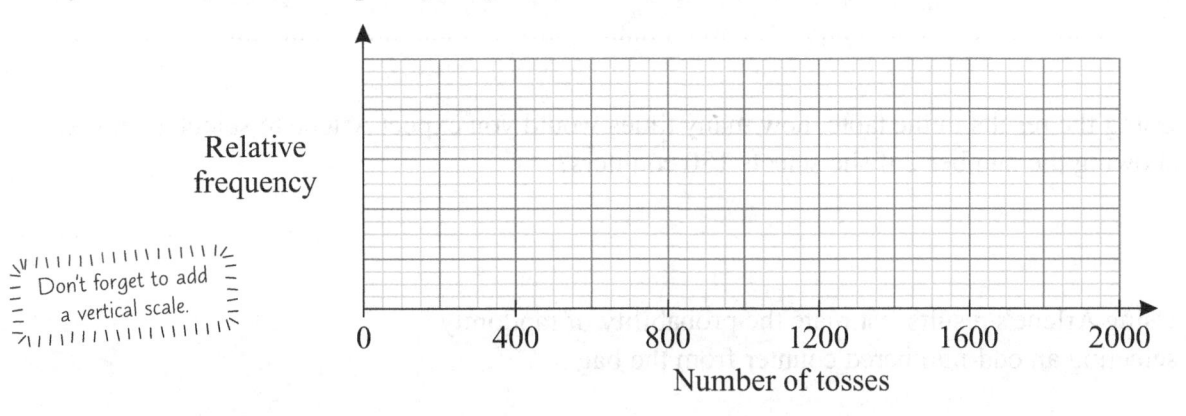

*Don't forget to add a vertical scale.*

[1]

b) If the coin were fair, how many times would you expect it to land on tails if it were tossed 1500 times?

..................

[2]

*[Total 3 marks]*

Section Four — Statistics

3   A parcel delivery company investigated the probability that any parcel was delivered late. The relative frequency of late parcels after the company had delivered a total of 200, 400, 600, 800 and 1000 parcels is shown on the graph below.

a) After 400 parcels were delivered, how many parcels were late?

...................
[2]

b) Which relative frequency from the graph should be the most accurate estimate? Explain your answer.

..................................................................
..................................................................
[1]

[Total 3 marks]

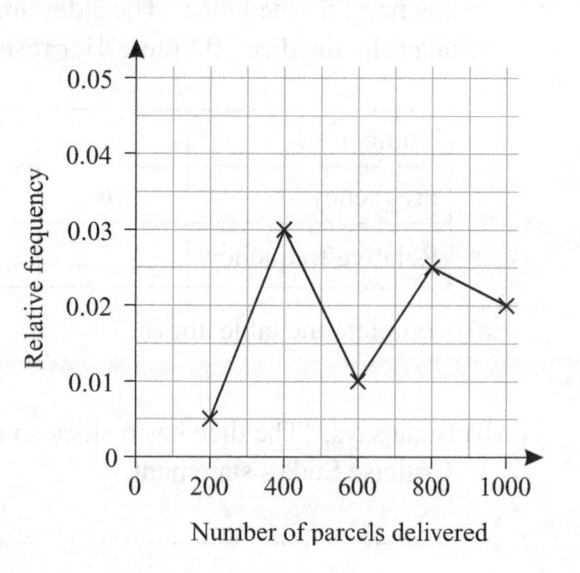

4   Arlene has a bag containing a large number of counters. Each counter is numbered either 1, 2, 3, 4 or 5.

She randomly selects one counter from the bag, makes a note of its number, and then puts it back in the bag. Arlene does this 100 times. She records her results in the table below.

| Number on counter | 1 | 2 | 3 | 4 | 5 |
|---|---|---|---|---|---|
| Frequency | 23 | 25 | 22 | 21 | 9 |
| Relative Frequency | | | | | |

a) Complete the table.
[2]

b) Arlene says that the bag contains the same number of counters with each number. Do you agree? Give a reason for your answer.

..................................................................
[1]

c) Using the results in the table, how many times would you expect Arlene to select a counter showing the number 2 if she selects 180 counters?

...................
[2]

d) Using Arlene's results, estimate the probability of randomly selecting an odd-numbered counter from the bag.

...................
[2]

[Total 7 marks]

# The And/Or Rules

1   A biased 5-sided spinner is numbered 1-5.

The probability that the spinner will land on each of the numbers 1 to 5 is given in this table.

| Number | 1 | 2 | 3 | 4 | 5 |
|---|---|---|---|---|---|
| Probability | 0.3 | 0.15 | 0.2 | 0.25 | 0.1 |

a) What is the probability of the spinner landing on a 4 or a 5?

....................
[2]

b) The spinner is spun twice. What is the probability that it will land on a 1 on the first spin and a 3 on the second spin?

....................
[2]

[Total 4 marks]

2   Shaun is playing the game 'hook-a-duck'.
   The probability that he wins a prize is 0.3.

a) What is the probability that he does not win a prize?

....................
[1]

b) If he plays two games, what is the probability that he doesn't win a prize in either game?

....................
[2]

[Total 3 marks]

3   Alisha and Anton are often late for dance class.
   The probability that Alisha is late is 0.9. The probability that Anton is late is 0.8.

What is the probability that at least 1 of them is late to the next dance class?

P(at least 1 is late) = 1 − P(neither is late)

P(Alisha isn't late) = 1 − ............ = ............    P(Anton isn't late) = 1 − ............ = ............

P(neither is late) = ............ × ............ = ............

P(at least 1 is late) = 1 − ............ = ............

....................
[Total 4 marks]

### Exam Practice Tip
Remember, if you're being asked the probability of Thing One AND Thing Two happening you MULTIPLY, and if you're being asked the probability of Thing One OR Thing Two happening you ADD. Be careful with your adding and multiplying if your probabilities are fractions — it's an easy way to slip up.

Score: 11

Section Four — Statistics

# Tree Diagrams

**1** The probability that Jo will wear a jumper to work is $\frac{2}{5}$.
The probability that Heather will wear a jumper to work is $\frac{1}{4}$.
The two events are independent.

a) Complete the tree diagram on the right.

[2]

b) What is the probability that neither Jo nor Heather wear a jumper?

.....................
[2]

[Total 4 marks]

**2** The Grizebeck Greys are a football team. The tree diagram below shows the probabilities of the weather conditions at their football ground on any chosen match day, and the probability of each possible result of a match.

a) Calculate the probability that on a randomly chosen match day, it will be wet and then the Grizebeck Greys will draw.

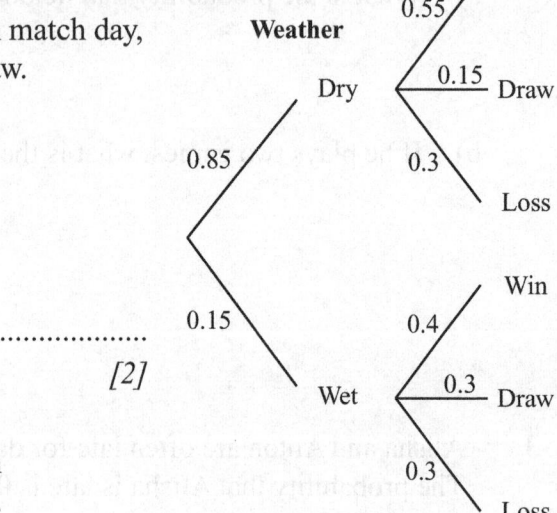

...................
[2]

b) Calculate the probability that on a randomly chosen match day, the Grizebeck Greys will win the match.

.........................
[3]

[Total 5 marks]

### Exam Practice Tip
To find the probability of an end result from a tree diagram, just multiply along the branches. If you want the total probability of more than one end result, add up the relevant probabilities (and remember that sometimes it's easier to find the probability of the thing you want not happening, then subtracting from 1).

Score: 9

Section Four — Statistics

# Probability from Venn Diagrams

**1** 27 workers in an office were asked if they liked digestives, cookies and ginger biscuits. 1 person didn't like any of the biscuits. The results are shown in the Venn diagram.

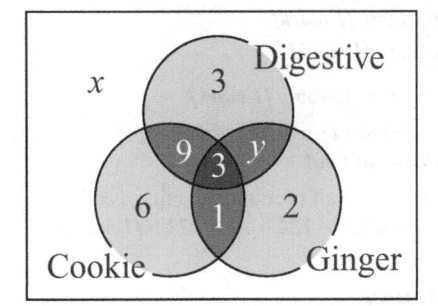

a) Find the values of $x$ and $y$ on the Venn diagram.

$x = $ .........................., $y = $ ..........................

[2]

b) What is the probability that a worker, chosen at random, likes cookies and digestives, but not ginger biscuits?

..........................

[2]

*[Total 4 marks]*

**2** The universal set, $\varepsilon = \{2, 3, 4, 5, 6, 7, 8, 9, 10\}$
Set A contains only even numbers and Set B contains only prime numbers.

a) Complete the Venn diagram by putting each number from $\varepsilon$ in the diagram.

[4]

b) Find the probability that a randomly selected number from $\varepsilon$ is either even or prime.

..........................

[2]

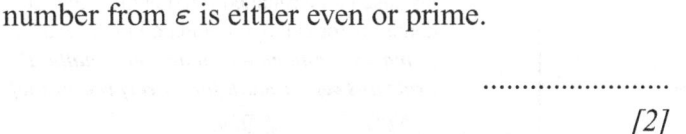

*[Total 6 marks]*

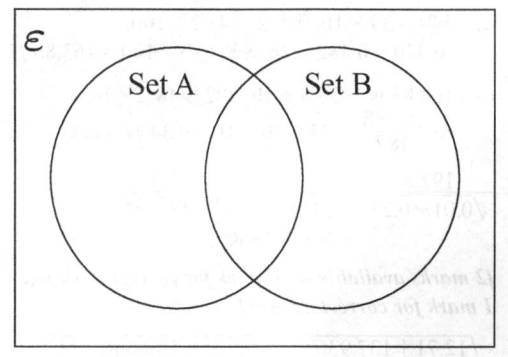

**3** A hot dog stand offers both ketchup and mustard as sauces for their hot dogs. One day the hot dog seller records the choices of a large number of customers. He finds that, of the people who bought a hot dog, a total of 14% had ketchup, a total of 8% had mustard and 2% had both.

a) Complete the Venn diagram to show this information.

[2]

b) Find the probability, as a fraction, that a customer had sauce on their hot dog.

..........................

[1]

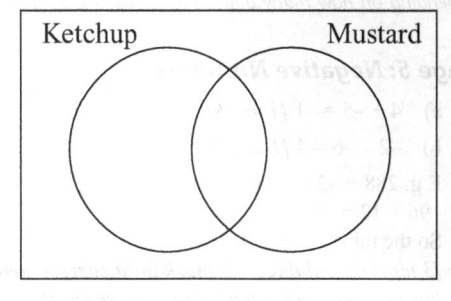

c) The following day, 275 customers buy a hot dog. Using the previous day's results, how many customers would the hot dog seller expect to have just ketchup?

..........................

[2]

*[Total 5 marks]*

Score: 15

Section Four — Statistics

# Answers

## Section One — Number

### Pages 3-4: Calculations and Operations

1. $0.8 \times 0.4 = 0.32$ *[1 mark]*

2. $\dfrac{4.2 \times 2.5}{9.1 - 5.9} = \dfrac{10.5}{3.2} = 3.28125$ *[1 mark]*

   Do this in stages — work out the top and the bottom of the fraction separately, then do the division.

3. a) $11 + 14 \div 2 = 11 + 7 = 18$
   *[2 marks available — 1 mark for doing the calculation steps in the correct order, 1 mark for the correct answer]*

   b) $(20 - 15) \times (4 + 6) = 5 \times 10 = 50$
   *[2 marks available — 1 mark for doing the calculation steps in the correct order, 1 mark for the correct answer]*

4. a) 4270 is 427 × 10, so 56 × 4270 = 23 912 × 10
   = 239 120 *[1 mark]*

   b) 42.7 is 427 ÷ 10, so $\dfrac{23\,912}{42.7} = 56 \times 10 = 560$ *[1 mark]*

   c) 5.6 is 56 ÷ 10, 4.27 is 427 ÷ 100,
   so 5.6 × 4.27 = 23 912 ÷ 10 ÷ 100 = 23.912 *[1 mark]*

5. a) 3.4 is 34 ÷ 10, 4.82 is 48.2 ÷ 10,
   so 3.4 × 4.82 = 1638.8 ÷ 10 ÷ 10 = 16.388 *[1 mark]*

   b) 340 is 34 × 10, 0.482 is 48.2 ÷ 100,
   so 340 × 0.482 = 1638.8 × 10 ÷ 100 = 163.88 *[1 mark]*

   c) 163.88 is 1638.8 ÷ 10, 482 is 48.2 × 10,
   so $\dfrac{163.88}{482} = 34 \div 10 \div 10 = 0.34$ *[1 mark]*

6. $\dfrac{197.8}{\sqrt{0.01 + 0.23}} = \dfrac{197.8}{\sqrt{0.24}} = \dfrac{197.8}{0.489897948...}$
   = 403.7575593
   *[2 marks available — 1 mark for correct working, 1 mark for correct answer]*

7. $\sqrt{\dfrac{12.71 + 137.936}{\cos 50° \times 13.2^2}} = \sqrt{\dfrac{150.646}{0.642787609... \times 174.24}}$
   $= \sqrt{1.34506182...}$
   = 1.159768003
   *[2 marks available — 1 mark for correct working, 1 mark for correct answer]*

Your answers to Q6 and Q7 might have a few more or fewer digits depending on how many digits your calculator is able to display.

### Page 5: Negative Numbers

1. a) $4 + -5 = -1$ *[1 mark]*
   b) $-2 - -6 = 4$ *[1 mark]*

2. E.g. $288 \div -3 = -96$
   $-96 \div 12 = -8$
   So the third number is $-8$
   *[3 marks available — 1 mark for a correct method, 1 mark for at least one correct calculation, 1 mark for the correct answer]*
   You could have worked out $-3 \times 12$ (= $-36$) and divided by this instead.

3. $-1.12, -0.61, -0.23, 0.35, 0.75, 1.06$ *[1 mark]*

4. $(3 - -4) \times 5 = 7 \times 5 = 35$
   *[3 marks available — 1 mark for (3 - -4), 1 mark for × 5, 1 mark for correct answer]*
   You might need to use trial and error for this one.

### Page 6: Rounding Numbers

1. a) 0.30 *[1 mark]*
   b) 0.303 *[1 mark]*

2. a) 428.6 light years *[1 mark]*
   b) 430 light years *[1 mark]*

3. $\dfrac{4.32^2 - \sqrt{13.4}}{16.3 + 2.19} = 0.8113466...$ *[1 mark]*
   = 0.811 (3 s.f.) *[1 mark]*
   *[2 marks available in total — as above]*

4. Rounding unit = 1, so half of rounding unit = 1 ÷ 2 = 0.5
   Smallest possible value = 122 − 0.5 = 121.5 *[1 mark]*

### Page 7: Estimating

1. E.g. Height of penguin ≈ 180 ÷ 3 *[1 mark]*
   = 60 cm (accept 50-67 cm) *[1 mark]*
   *[2 marks available in total — as above]*

2. E.g. $\dfrac{12.2 \times 1.86}{0.19} \approx \dfrac{10 \times 2}{0.2} = \dfrac{20}{0.2} = 100$
   *[2 marks available — 1 mark for rounding to suitable values, 1 mark for the correct final answer using your values]*
   If you rounded differently you might get a different answer, but as long as your rounding is sensible you'll get the marks.

3. a) $\dfrac{215.7 \times 44.8}{460} \approx \dfrac{200 \times 40}{500} = \dfrac{8000}{500} = 16$
   *[2 marks available — 1 mark for rounding to 1 s.f., 1 mark for the correct final answer]*

   b) The answer to a) will be smaller than the exact answer, because in the rounded fraction the numerator is smaller and denominator is larger compared to the exact calculation.
   *[2 marks available — 1 mark for 'smaller than the exact answer', 1 mark for correct reasoning]*

4. $\sqrt{\dfrac{2321}{19.673 \times 3.81}} \approx \sqrt{\dfrac{2000}{20 \times 4}}$
   *[1 mark for rounding sensibly]*
   $= \sqrt{\dfrac{100}{4}} = \sqrt{25}$ *[1 mark for either expression]*
   = 5 *[1 mark]*
   *[3 marks available in total — as above]*
   You might have a different answer if you've rounded differently — as long as your rounding is sensible, you'll get the marks.

### Page 8: Bounds

1. Minimum weight = 56.5 kg *[1 mark]*
   Maximum weight = 57.5 kg *[1 mark]*
   *[2 marks available in total — as above]*

2. a) 54.05 cm *[1 mark]*
   b) lower bound for the width of the paper = 23.55 cm *[1 mark]*
   lower bound for the perimeter
   = (54.05 cm × 2) + (23.55 cm × 2) = 155.2 cm *[1 mark]*
   *[2 marks available in total — as above]*

3   Upper bound of $x$ = 2.25 *[1 mark]*
    So upper bound of $4x + 3 = 4 \times 2.25 + 3 = 12$
    Lower bound of $x$ = 2.15 *[1 mark]*
    So lower bound of $4x + 3 = 4 \times 2.15 + 3 = 11.6$
    Written as an interval, this is $11.6 \leq 4x + 3 < 12$
    *[2 marks — 1 for both bounds correct,
    1 mark for expressing as an inequality correctly]*
    *[4 marks available in total — as above]*

4   Lower bound of difference = 13.65 – 8.35 *[1 mark]*
    = 5.3 litres *[1 mark]*
    *[2 marks available in total — as above]*

## Page 9: Special Types of Number

1   a) 100 *[1 mark]*
    b) 27 *[1 mark]*

2   a) $4^3 + 6^2 = 64 + 36 = 100$
    *[2 marks available — 1 mark for either 64 or 36,
    1 mark for the correct answer]*
    b) $5^2 \times 3^2 = 25 \times 9 = 225$
    *[2 marks available — 1 mark for either 25 or 9,
    1 mark for the correct answer]*
    c) $\sqrt{81} - 2^2 = 9 - 4 = 5$
    *[2 marks available — 1 mark for either 9 or 4,
    1 mark for the correct answer]*

3   True.
    E.g. Two consecutive integers will always be an even number and an odd number, and adding an even and an odd number always gives an odd number.
    *[2 marks available — 1 mark for circling 'True' and 1 mark for a correct explanation]*

## Pages 10-11: Multiples, Factors and Prime Factors

1   E.g. 37 (3 + 7 = 10, which is 1 more than 9, a square number)
    *[2 marks available — 2 marks for a correct answer, otherwise 1 mark for a prime of two or more digits]*

2   a) 1, 2, 4, 7, 14, 28
    *[2 marks available — 2 marks if all 6 factors are correct and no extra incorrect factors have been included, otherwise 1 mark if all 6 factors are correct but 1 extra incorrect factor has been included, or if at least 4 factors are correct and there are no more than 6 numbers listed in total]*
    b) 56, 64 *[1 mark]*

3   Any **two** from 1, 2, 3, 4, 6 and 12.
    *[2 marks available — 1 mark for each correct common factor]*

4   a) $2 \times 3 \times 5 \times 7$
    *[2 marks available — 2 marks for the correct answer, otherwise 1 mark if they've found two correct factors]*
    b) $3^2 \times 5^2 \times 7^2$
    *[2 marks available — 1 mark for a correct method, 1 mark for all prime factors correct]*

5   E.g. take $a = 2$ and $b = 3$.
    a) 2 + 3 = 5 *[1 mark]*
    b) $2 \times 3 = 6$ *[1 mark]*
    c) $2^2 + 3^2 = 4 + 9 = 13$ *[1 mark]*
    You could use different numbers for a and b, but one of them will always need to be 2 and the other will always need to be odd.

6   E.g. 4 (even) has three factors (1, 2 and 4).
    81 (odd) has five factors (1, 3, 9, 27 and 81).
    *[2 marks available — 1 mark for each correct example of odd and even square numbers with a suitable number of factors.]*
    These aren't the only square numbers that would work here — any pair where the odd number doesn't have fewer factors than the even number would get you the marks.

7   Common multiples of 6 and 7:
    42, 84, 126, 168, 210, 252, ... *[1 mark]*
    Factors of 252: 1, 2, 3, 4, 6, 7, 9, 12, 14, 18, 21, 28, 36, 42, 63, 84, 126, 252
    Factors of 420: 1, 2, 3, 4, 5, 6, 7, 10, 12, 14, 15, 20, 21, 28, 30, 35, 42, 60, 70, 84, 105, 140, 210, 420 *[1 mark for both sets of factors]*
    Common factors of 252 and 420:
    1, 2, 3, 4, 6, 7, 12, 14, 21, 28, 42, 84 *[1 mark]*
    So $x = 84$ *[1 mark]*
    *[4 marks available in total — as above]*

## Page 12: HCF and LCM

1   a) LCM = $3^7 \times 7^3 \times 11^2$ *[1 mark]*
    b) HCF = $3^4 \times 11$ *[1 mark]*

2   a) LCM = $2^8 \times 5^3 \times 7$
    *[2 marks available — 2 marks for the correct answer, otherwise 1 mark for a common multiple of all three numbers]*
    b) HCF = $2^5$
    *[2 marks available — 2 marks for the correct answer, otherwise 1 mark for a common factor of all three numbers]*

3   Prime factorisation of $A = A$
    Prime factorisation of $B = B$ (as $A$ and $B$ are prime)
    So LCM = $A \times B$ (or $AB$)
    *[2 marks available — 2 marks for the correct answer, otherwise 1 mark for stating that the prime factorisations of A and B are A and B]*

## Pages 13-14: Fractions

1   a) $(60 \div 5) \times 3 = 12 \times 3 = 36$
    *[2 marks available — 1 mark for dividing by 5 or multiplying by 3, 1 mark for the correct answer]*
    b) $\frac{15}{40} = \frac{3}{8}$
    *[2 marks available — 1 mark for putting the numbers into a fraction, 1 mark for the correct final answer]*

2   a) $\frac{1}{2} \times \frac{1}{6} = \frac{1 \times 1}{2 \times 6} = \frac{1}{12}$ *[1 mark]*
    b) $\frac{2}{3} \div \frac{3}{5} = \frac{2}{3} \times \frac{5}{3} = \frac{2 \times 5}{3 \times 3} = \frac{10}{9}$ or $1\frac{1}{9}$
    *[2 marks available — 1 mark for changing to the reciprocal fraction and multiplying, 1 mark for the correct answer]*

3   $\frac{5}{6} = \frac{20}{24}$, $\frac{3}{4} = \frac{18}{24}$, $\frac{7}{8} = \frac{21}{24}$
    All these fractions are less than one, and the largest is $\frac{21}{24}$,
    so the fraction closest to 1 is $\frac{7}{8}$ *[1 mark]*

4   $\frac{1}{3} \times 3 = 1$, so there are three thirds in 1. $3 \times 12 = 36$.
    So there are 36 thirds in 12 *[1 mark]*.

5   Shaded regions are $\frac{1}{4}$, $\frac{1}{4} \times \frac{1}{4} = \frac{1}{16}$ and $\frac{1}{4} \times \frac{1}{4} \times \frac{1}{4} = \frac{1}{64}$
    So total area shaded = $\frac{1}{4} + \frac{1}{16} + \frac{1}{64} = \frac{16}{64} + \frac{4}{64} + \frac{1}{64} = \frac{21}{64}$
    *[3 marks available — 1 mark for working out the fraction for each shaded region, 1 mark for writing over a common denominator, 1 mark for correct answer]*

6   a) $\frac{4}{12} + \frac{3}{5} = \frac{20}{60} + \frac{36}{60} = \frac{56}{60} = \frac{14}{15}$
    *[2 marks available — 1 mark for writing over a common denominator, 1 mark for simplifying]*
    b) $\frac{9}{10} - \frac{2}{8} = \frac{36}{40} - \frac{10}{40} = \frac{26}{40} = \frac{13}{20}$
    *[2 marks available — 1 mark for writing over a common denominator, 1 mark for simplifying]*

7   a) $3\frac{1}{2} + 2\frac{3}{5} = \frac{7}{2} + \frac{13}{5} = \frac{35}{10} + \frac{26}{10} = \frac{35+26}{10} = \frac{61}{10}$ or $6\frac{1}{10}$

*[3 marks available — 1 mark for writing as improper fractions, 1 mark for writing over a common denominator, 1 mark for the correct answer]*

   b) $3\frac{3}{4} - 2\frac{1}{3} = \frac{15}{4} - \frac{7}{3} = \frac{45}{12} - \frac{28}{12} = \frac{45-28}{12} = \frac{17}{12}$ or $1\frac{5}{12}$

*[3 marks available — 1 mark for writing as improper fractions, 1 mark for writing over a common denominator, 1 mark for the correct answer]*

*If you've used a different method in Q7, but still shown your working, and ended up with the same final answer, then you still get full marks.*

## Pages 15-16: Fractions, Decimals and Percentages

1   a) $\frac{3}{5} = \frac{6}{10} = 0.6$ *[1 mark]*
    b) $0.04 \times 100 = 4\%$ *[1 mark]*
    c) $65\% = \frac{65}{100}$
       $= \frac{65 \div 5}{100 \div 5} = \frac{13}{20}$ *[1 mark]*

2   $65\% = 0.65$, $\frac{2}{3} = 0.666...$, $\frac{33}{50} = 0.66$
    So order is 0.065, 65%, $\frac{33}{50}$, $\frac{2}{3}$

*[3 marks available — 3 marks for all four amounts in the correct order, otherwise 2 marks for correctly writing all four amounts in the same form (fraction, decimal or percentage), or 1 mark for attempting to write all amounts in the correct form but with one incorrect amount]*

3   Convert $\frac{8}{25}$ to a percentage:
    $\frac{8}{25} = \frac{8 \times 4}{25 \times 4} = \frac{32}{100} = 32\%$ *[1 mark]*
    $100\% - (42\% + 32\%) = 100\% - 74\% = 26\%$ *[1 mark]*
    So 26% of the blocks are green.
    $100\% = 150$, $10\% = 15$, $1\% = 1.5$
    $26\% = 20\% + 6\%$
    $= (2 \times 15) + (6 \times 1.5)$
    $= 30 + 9 = 39$ blocks are green. *[1 mark]*
*[3 marks available in total — as above]*

4   $10 \div 11 = 0.9\dot{0}$ *[1 mark]*

5   $1 \div 0.3 = 3.3333... = 3.3$ (1 d.p.) *[1 mark]*

6   $25\% = \frac{1}{4}$, so 25% of $\frac{1}{5} = \frac{1}{4} \times \frac{1}{5} = \frac{1}{20}$ *[1 mark]*

7   $\frac{1}{4} = 25\%$, so the first person pays $1 - 25\% - 20\% - 20\%$
    $= 1 - 65\% = 35\%$ *[1 mark]*
    £17.50 = 35% *[1 mark]*, so 1% = £17.50 ÷ 35 = £0.50.
    The total bill was £0.50 × 100 *[1 mark]* = £50 *[1 mark]*.
*[4 marks available — as above]*

## Pages 17-18: Percentages

1   100% of 5200 = 5200
    10% of 5200 = 5200 ÷ 10 = 520
    5% of 5200 = 520 ÷ 2 = 260
    115% = 5200 + 520 + 260 = 5980
*[2 marks available — 1 mark for a correct method, 1 mark for the correct answer]*

2   $\frac{18}{60} = \frac{3}{10} = 30\%$ *[1 mark]*

3   7% = 7 ÷ 100 = 0.07,
    0.07 × £150 = £10.50 interest per year *[1 mark]*
    £10.50 × 3 = £31.50 interest after 3 years *[1 mark]*.
*[2 marks available in total — as above]*
*Remember that simple interest just adds interest to the initial amount. So in this case, there are 3 lots of interest all on the initial £150. In contrast, compound interest would add interest onto any interest that's been added in previous years.*

4   20% = 20 ÷ 100 = 0.2
    0.2 × £927 = £185.40 *[1 mark]*
    £927 + £185.40 = £1112.40 *[1 mark]*
*[2 marks available in total — as above]*
*In questions about percentage increase and decrease, you could also use the multiplier method. If you used this method, you would get a mark for trying to use the correct multiplier.*

5   £15 714 = 108%
    £15 714 ÷ 108 = £145.50 = 1% *[1 mark]*
    £145.50 × 100 = 100% = £14 550 *[1 mark]*
*[2 marks available in total — as above]*

6   13 104 = 117%
    13 104 ÷ 117 = 112 = 1% *[1 mark]*
    112 × 100 = 100% = 11 200 *[1 mark]*
*[2 marks available in total — as above]*

7   Let the original price of the TV be £100.
    The sale price of the TV is then 0.8 × 100 = £80 *[1 mark]*
    After the sale event, the price of the TV increases by
    £100 − £80 = £20 *[1 mark]*
    $\frac{20}{80} = \frac{1}{4} = 25\%$ *[1 mark]*
*[3 marks available in total — as above]*
*You could use any number for the original price of the TV, or even just 'x' — the sale price would then be £0.8x and the increase in price is £0.2x. As long as you show correct working, you'll still get full marks.*

8   15% of $a$ is $0.15a$
    The number of balls left in bag $A$ is $0.85a$. *[1 mark]*
    The number of balls then in bag $B$ is $b + 0.15a$. *[1 mark]*
    $0.85a = b + 0.15a$ *[1 mark]*
    $0.7a = b$, so $b$ is 70% of $a$. *[1 mark]*
*[4 marks available in total — as above]*

## Pages 19-20: Compound Growth and Decay

1   Multiplier = 1 + 0.06 = 1.06
    After 3 years the amount will be: £750 × (1.06)³ = £893.262
    = £893.26 (to the nearest penny)
*[3 marks available — 1 mark for working out the multiplier, 1 mark for a correct method, 1 mark for the correct answer]*

2   a) When it was first opened $t = 0$, so the balance would have been $B = 5000 \times 1.02^0 = 5000 \times 1 = £5000$ *[1 mark]*
    b) After 7 years there would be:
       $B = 5000 \times 1.02^7$ *[1 mark]*
       = £5743.4283...
       = £5743.43 (to the nearest penny) *[1 mark]*
*[2 marks available in total — as above]*

3   10% increase = 1 + 0.1 = 1.1 *[1 mark]*
    After 5 km, the car will be travelling at $30 \times 1.1^5$ *[1 mark]*
    = 48.3153 = 48.3 km/h (3 s.f.) *[1 mark]*
*[3 marks available in total — as above]*

4   Multiplier = 1 − 0.25 = 0.75 *[1 mark]*
    10 000 × (0.75)⁵ = 2373.0468...
             = £2373 (to the nearest pound) *[1 mark]*
*[2 marks available in total — as above]*

5   a) Compound Interest Account:
       Multiplier = 1 + 0.055 = 1.055 *[1 mark]*
       £10 000 × (1.055)⁵ = £13 069.60 (2 d.p.) *[1 mark]*
       Simple Interest Account:
       6.2% of £10 000 = 0.062 × £10 000 = £620 *[1 mark]*
       5 × £620 = £3100
       £10 000 + £3100 = £13 100 so they should put the money in the Simple Interest Account to get the biggest returns after 5 years. *[1 mark]*
*[4 marks available in total — as above]*
    b) E.g. They might want to deposit more money during the 5 years and they can't with the Simple Interest Account. *[1 mark]*

Answers

6  5000 × 0.16 = 800 trees are planted in 2016 *[1 mark]*.
   A maximum of 800 × 0.75 = 600 trees are cut down.
   At the end of 2016 there is a minimum of
   5000 + (800 − 600) = 5200 pine trees *[1 mark]*
   5200 × 0.16 = 832 trees are planted in 2017 *[1 mark]*.
   A maximum of 832 × 0.75 = 624 trees are cut down.
   At the end of 2017 there is a minimum of
   5200 + (832 − 624) = 5408 pine trees *[1 mark]*.
   *[4 marks available in total — as above]*

## Pages 21-22: Ratios

1  16 : 240 = (16 ÷ 8) : (240 ÷ 8) = 2 : 30 = 1 : 15
   *[2 marks available — 2 marks for a fully simplified answer, otherwise 1 mark for any correct simplification]*

2  a) There are 4 + 3 + 7 = 14 parts in total and 3 of them are pineapple juice.
      $\frac{3}{14}$ of the fruit punch is pineapple juice. *[1 mark]*
   b) 700 ÷ (4 + 3 + 7) = 700 ÷ 14
                        = 50 ml per part
      Apple juice: 50 × 4 = 200 ml
      Pineapple juice : 50 × 3 = 150 ml
      Cherryade: 50 × 7 = 350 ml
      *[3 marks available — 1 mark for dividing 700 by the sum of the numbers in the ratio, 1 mark for multiplying this value by each number in the ratio, 1 mark if all three quantities are correct]*
      You might have worked this out using fractions — this method is fine, but check that your final answers match those in this solution.

3  84 ÷ (3 + 5 + 4 + 8) = 84 ÷ 20 *[1 mark]*
                        = 4.2
   Largest share is 8 × 4.2 = 33.6 *[1 mark]*
   *[2 marks available in total — as above]*

4  Catrin, Ariana, Nasir and Rhonda shared the money in the ratio 1 : 2 : 4 : 8 *[1 mark for 1 : 2 : 4 : 8 or an equivalent ratio (order may be different)]*
   660 ÷ (1 + 2 + 4 + 8) = 44 *[1 mark]*
   Rhonda got £44 × 8 = £352 *[1 mark]*
   *[3 marks available in total — as above]*
   You could answer this question using a formula — if you let x be the amount of money that Catrin gets, then x + 2x + 4x + 8x = £660.

5  The largest piece is 7 parts, the smallest piece is 3 parts.
   300 g = 7 parts − 3 parts = 4 parts *[1 mark]*
   1 part = 300 g ÷ 4 = 75 g *[1 mark]*
   There are a total of 3 + 6 + 7 = 16 parts *[1 mark]*
   The total weight of the block of wood is 75 g × 16 = 1200 g
   *[1 mark]*
   *[4 marks available in total — as above]*

6  Ratio of red : green is 1 : 3 = 4 : 12 and ratio of green : white is 4 : 3 = 12 : 9 *[1 mark]*
   So ratio of red : green : white = 4 : 12 : 9 *[1 mark]*
   The fraction of the tiles that are white is $\frac{9}{4+12+9} = \frac{9}{25}$
   *[1 mark]*
   *[3 marks available in total — as above]*

## Page 23: Direct and Inverse Proportion

1  1 T-shirt will take: 5 m² ÷ 8 = 0.625 m² of cotton *[1 mark]*
   85 T-shirts will take: 0.625 m² × 85 = 53.125 m² of cotton *[1 mark]*
   1 m² of cotton costs: £5.50 ÷ 2 = £2.75 *[1 mark]*
   53.125 m² of cotton costs £2.75 × 53.125 = £146.09375
                                            = £146.09 *[1 mark]*
   *[4 marks available in total — as above]*

2  To harvest the same amount as Neil, Sian will take:
   3.5 hours ÷ 2 = 1.75 hours *[1 mark]*
   Sian needs to harvest three times as much so it will take her:
   1.75 × 3 *[1 mark]* = 5.25 hours *[1 mark]*
   *[3 marks available in total — as above]*

3  a) 1 litre of petrol will keep 8 go-karts going for:
      20 ÷ 12 = 1.666... minutes *[1 mark]*
      18 litres of petrol will keep 8 go-karts going for:
      1.666... × 18 = 30 minutes *[1 mark]*
      18 litres of petrol will keep 1 go-kart going for:
      30 × 8 = 240 minutes *[1 mark]*
      18 litres of petrol will keep 6 go-karts going for:
      240 ÷ 6 = 40 minutes *[1 mark]*
      *[4 marks available in total — as above]*
      You might have done these steps in a slightly different order — you'd still get all the marks as long as you got the same answer.
   b) In 1 minute, 8 go-karts will use 12 ÷ 20 = 0.6 litres *[1 mark]*
      In 45 minutes, 8 go-karts will use 0.6 × 45 = 27 litres *[1 mark]*
      27 litres of petrol cost: £1.37 × 27 = £36.99 *[1 mark]*
      *[3 marks available in total — as above]*

## Page 24: Powers and Roots

1  a) $8.7^3 = 658.503$ *[1 mark]*
   b) $\sqrt[3]{729} = 9$ *[1 mark]*
   c) $4^{-2} = 0.0625$ *[1 mark]*

2  $\frac{3^4 \times 3^7}{3^6} = \frac{3^{(4+7)}}{3^6} = \frac{3^{11}}{3^6} = 3^{(11-6)} = 3^5$
   *[2 marks available — 1 mark for a correct attempt at adding or subtracting powers, 1 mark for the correct final answer]*

3  a) $3^0 = 1$ *[1 mark]*
   b) $8^{\frac{1}{3}} = \sqrt[3]{8} = 2$ *[1 mark]*

4  $(2^4 \times 2^7) = 2^{(4+7)} = 2^{11}$
   $(2^3 \times 2^2) = 2^{(3+2)} = 2^5$, so $(2^3 \times 2^2)^2 = (2^5)^2 = 2^{10}$
   So $(2^4 \times 2^7) \div (2^3 \times 2^2)^2 = 2^{11} \div 2^{10} = 2^1 = 2$
   *[2 marks available — 1 mark if each bracket has been correctly simplified, 1 mark for the correct answer]*

## Pages 25-26: Standard Form

1  a) $A = 4.834 \times 10^9 = 4\,834\,000\,000$ *[1 mark]*
   b) $B \times C = (2.7 \times 10^5) \times 5800$
              $= (2.7 \times 10^5) \times (5.8 \times 10^3) = (2.7 \times 5.8) \times (10^5 \times 10^3)$
              $= 15.66 \times 10^8$ *[1 mark]*
              $= 1.566 \times 10^9$ *[1 mark]*
      *[2 marks available in total — as above]*
   c) $C, B, A$ ($5800 = 5.8 \times 10^3$, $2.7 \times 10^5$, $4.834 \times 10^9$) *[1 mark]*

2  a) $6.482 \times 10^8$ *[1 mark]*
   b) $2.45 \times 10^{-5}$ *[1 mark]*

3  $(9.3 \times 10^7) \div (1.86 \times 10^5) = 5 \times 10^2$
   *[2 marks available — 2 marks for the correct answer, otherwise 1 mark if the final answer has the correct value (500), but has not been written correctly in standard form]*

4  $A = (5 \times 10^5) + (5 \times 10^3) + (5 \times 10^2) + (5 \times 10^{-2})$
      $= 500\,000 + 5000 + 500 + 0.05$ *[1 mark]*
      $= 505\,500.05$ *[1 mark]*
   *[2 marks available in total — as above]*

5  $A : B = 1.5 \times 10^8 : 4.5 \times 10^9$
   $(4.5 \times 10^9) \div (1.5 \times 10^8) = (4.5 \div 1.5) \times (10^9 \div 10^8)$ *[1 mark]*
   $= 3 \times 10^1 = 30$ *[1 mark]*. So the ratio is 1 : 30 *[1 mark]*
   *[3 marks available in total — as above]*

6  a) $(4 \times 10^{-4}) \div (8 \times 10^{-5}) = (4 \div 8) \times (10^{-4} \div 10^{-5})$
      $= 0.5 \times 10^1$ *[1 mark]*
      $= 5$ *[1 mark]*
      *[2 marks available in total — as above]*
   b) $4 \times 10^{-4} + 6 \times 10^{-5} = 4 \times 10^{-4} + 0.6 \times 10^{-4}$
      $= (4 + 0.6) \times 10^{-4} = 4.6 \times 10^{-4}$
      *[2 marks available — 2 marks for the correct answer, otherwise 1 mark if the final answer has the correct value, but has not been written correctly in standard form]*
      You could have done this one by turning $4 \times 10^{-4}$ into $40 \times 10^{-5}$ and adding it to $6 \times 10^{-5}$ instead — but you'd need to convert to standard form at the end.

7  $7.59 \times 10^7 + 2.1 \times 10^5 = 7.611 \times 10^7$
   *[2 marks available — 2 marks for the correct answer, otherwise 1 mark if the final answer has the correct value, but has not been written correctly in standard form]*

## Page 27: Venn Diagrams

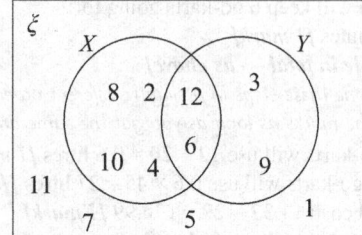

1  a)

   ξ, X, Y; X only: 8, 2, 10, 4; intersection: 12, 6; Y only: 3, 9; outside: 11, 7, 5, 1

   *[4 marks available — 4 marks for all numbers placed correctly and no extra numbers, otherwise 3 marks for 9 or more correct, 2 marks for 7 or more correct or 1 mark for 5 or more correct]*
   b) 2 *[1 mark]*
   c) 4 *[1 mark]*

2  a)

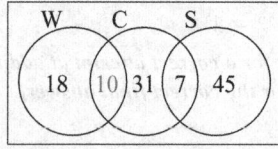

   W, C, S; 18, 10, 31, 7, 45

   *[2 marks available — 2 marks for all 4 numbers correct, otherwise 1 mark for 2 or 3 numbers correct]*
   b) $18 + 10 + 31 + 7 + 45 = 111$ customers *[1 mark]*

# Section Two — Algebra

## Page 28: Simplifying Terms

1  $10s$ *[1 mark]*
2  a) $4p$ *[1 mark]*
   b) $2m$ *[1 mark]*
   c) $4p + 3r$
      *[2 marks available — 1 mark for $4p$, 1 mark for $3r$]*
3  a) $10ab$ *[1 mark]*
   b) $4pq$ *[1 mark]*
   c) $x^2 + 4x$
      *[2 marks available — 1 mark for $x^2$, 1 mark for $4x$]*
4  $8 - x$
   *[2 marks available — 1 mark for 8, 1 mark for $-x$]*

## Page 29: Expanding Brackets

1  a) $3(x - 1) = (3 \times x) + (3 \times -1) = 3x - 3$ *[1 mark]*
   b) $4a(a + 2b) = (4a \times a) + (4a \times 2b) = 4a^2 + 8ab$ *[1 mark]*
   c) $8p^2(3 - 2p) - 2p(p - 3)$
      $= [(8p^2 \times 3) + (8p^2 \times -2p)] - [(2p \times p) + (2p \times -3)]$
      $= 24p^2 - 16p^3 - 2p^2 + 6p$ *[1 mark]*
      $= 22p^2 - 16p^3 + 6p$ *[1 mark]*
      *[2 marks available in total — as above]*

2  $a = 4(3b - 1) + 6(5 - 2b)$
   $a = (4 \times 3b) + (4 \times -1) + (6 \times 5) + (6 \times -2b)$
   $a = 12b - 4 + 30 - 12b$
   $a = 26$
   *[2 marks available — 1 mark for correctly expanding the brackets, 1 mark for simplifying to $a = 26$]*

3  a) $(2t - 5)(3t + 4) = (2t \times 3t) + (2t \times 4) + (-5 \times 3t) + (-5 \times 4)$
      $= 6t^2 + 8t - 15t - 20$
      $= 6t^2 - 7t - 20$
      *[2 marks available — 2 marks for the correct answer, otherwise 1 mark for $6t^2 + kt - 20$ or $6t^2 - 7t + k$ with an incorrect k]*
   b) $(x + 3)^2 = (x + 3)(x + 3)$
      $= (x \times x) + (x \times 3) + (3 \times x) + (3 \times 3)$
      $= x^2 + 3x + 3x + 9$
      $= x^2 + 6x + 9$
      *[2 marks available — 2 marks for the correct answer, otherwise 1 mark for $x^2 + kx + 9$ or $x^2 + 6x + k$ with an incorrect k]*

4  Area $= \frac{1}{2} \times$ base $\times$ height
   $= \frac{1}{2} \times (3x + 5) \times (2x - 4) = \frac{1}{2} (3x + 5)(2x - 4)$ *[1 mark]*
   $= \frac{1}{2} \times [(3x \times 2x) + (3x \times -4) + (5 \times 2x) + (5 \times -4)]$
   $= \frac{1}{2} \times (6x^2 - 12x + 10x - 20)$
   $= \frac{1}{2} \times (6x^2 - 2x - 20)$ *[1 mark]*
   $= 3x^2 - x - 10$ *[1 mark]*
   *[3 marks available in total — as above]*
   You could also have multiplied $(2x - 4)$ by $\frac{1}{2}$ first of all. The area would then just be $(3x + 5)(x - 2)$, which is a bit simpler to multiply out.

## Page 30: Factorising

1  a) $6x + 3 = (3 \times 2x) + (3 \times 1) = 3(2x + 1)$ *[1 mark]*
   b) $x(x + 7)$ *[1 mark]*
   c) $5(5p - 3q)$ *[1 mark]*
2  $8a^2 - 48ab = 8(a^2 - 6ab)$
   $= 8a(a - 6b)$
   *[2 marks available — 2 marks for a complete factorisation, otherwise 1 mark for a partial factorisation]*

3  a)  $16x + 4x^2 = 4(4x + x^2) = 4x(4 + x)$
       *[2 marks available — 2 marks for a complete factorisation, otherwise 1 mark for a partial factorisation]*
    b)  $25y^2 - 40y^3 = 5(5y^2 - 8y^3)$
                      $= 5y^2(5 - 8y)$
       *[2 marks available — 2 marks for a complete factorisation, otherwise 1 mark for a partial factorisation]*
    c)  $6v^2w^3 + 30v^4w^2 = 6(v^2w^3 + 5v^4w^2)$
                            $= 6v^2w^2(w + 5v^2)$
       *[2 marks available — 2 marks for a complete factorisation, otherwise 1 mark for a partial factorisation]*

## Page 31: Expressions and Formulas

1  a)  $S = 4m^2 + 2.5n$
       $S = (4 \times 2 \times 2) + (2.5 \times 10)$
       $S = 16 + 25 = 41$
       *[2 marks available — 2 marks for the correct answer, otherwise 1 mark for 16 or 25]*
    b)  $S = 4m^2 + 2.5n$
       $179 = (4 \times 6.5 \times 6.5) + (2.5 \times n)$
       $179 = 169 + 2.5n$ so $n = \frac{179 - 169}{2.5}$ *[1 mark]*
       $\Rightarrow n = 4$ *[1 mark]*
       *[2 marks available in total — as above]*

2  a)  an expression *[1 mark]*
    b)  an equation *[1 mark]*

3  a)  $23 + 7 = 30$
       $30 \div 5 = 6$, so when $x = 23$, $y = 6$ *[1 mark]*
    b)  $3 \times 5 = 15$
       $15 - 7 = 8$, so when $y = 3$, $x = 8$
       *[2 marks available — 1 mark for reversing the function machine, 1 mark for the correct value of x]*

## Page 32: Solving Equations

1  a)  $7b - 5 = 3(b + 1)$
       $7b - 5 = 3b + 3$ *[1 mark]*
       $7b - 3b = 3 + 5$
       $4b = 8$ *[1 mark]*
       $b = 8 \div 4 = 2$ *[1 mark]*
       *[3 marks available in total — as above]*
    b)  $\frac{45 - z}{5} = 6$
       $45 - z = 30$ *[1 mark]*
       $z = 45 - 30 = 15$ *[1 mark]*
       *[2 marks available in total — as above]*

2  $\frac{5 - 3x}{2} + \frac{6x + 1}{5} = 15$
   $\frac{2 \times 5 \times (5 - 3x)}{2} + \frac{2 \times 5 \times (6x + 1)}{5} = 150$
   $5(5 - 3x) + 2(6x + 1) = 150$ *[1 mark]*
   $25 - 15x + 12x + 2 = 150$ *[1 mark]*
   $-15x + 12x = 150 - 25 - 2$
   $-3x = 123$ *[1 mark]*
   $x = -41$ *[1 mark]*
   *[4 marks available in total — as above]*

3  The perimeter is $(3x - 4) + (x + 3) + (14 - x) + (4x + 5)$, so...
   $(3x - 4) + (x + 3) + (14 - x) + (4x + 5) = 67$ *[1 mark]*
   $7x + 18 = 67$ *[1 mark]*
   $7x = 67 - 18$
   $7x = 49$ *[1 mark]*
   $x = 7$ *[1 mark]*
   *[4 marks available in total — as above]*

## Page 33: Formulas and Equations from Words

1  a)  $A = 3x \times 3x$
       $A = 9x^2$ *[1 mark]*
    b)  $A = 9 \times 4^2 = 144$ cm² *[1 mark]*

2  a)  $C = 10p + e$ *[1 mark]*
    b)  Total number of items eaten, $e = 4 \times 8 = 32$
       $C = (10 \times 4) + 32$ *[1 mark]*
       $= £72$ *[1 mark]*
       *[2 marks available in total — as above]*

3  a)  The amount that Morgana paid is given by $\frac{T}{2}$.
       The amount that Iona paid is $3 + 0.5d$.
       If they paid the same amount, then $3 + 0.5d = \frac{T}{2}$. *[1 mark]*
    b)  $\frac{T}{2} = 3 + 0.5d$, so $T = 6 + d$ *[1 mark]*
       When $d = 2$, $T = 6 + 2 = 8$, so cost = £8 *[1 mark]*
       *[2 marks available in total — as above]*

## Page 34: Rearranging Formulas

1  a)  $u = v - at$ *[1 mark]*
    b)  $v - u = at$ *[1 mark]*
       $t = \frac{v - u}{a}$ *[1 mark]*
       *[2 marks available in total — as above]*

2  $\frac{a + 2}{3} = b - 1$
   $a + 2 = 3b - 3$ *[1 mark]*
   $a = 3b - 5$ *[1 mark]*
   *[2 marks available in total — as above]*

3  $x = y^2 - 7$
   $x + 7 = y^2$ *[1 mark]*
   $y = \pm\sqrt{x + 7}$ *[1 mark]*
   *[2 marks available in total — as above]*

4  $u = 2 + \frac{1}{w}$
   $u - 2 = \frac{1}{w}$ *[1 mark]*
   $w(u - 2) = 1$ *[1 mark]*
   $w = \frac{1}{u - 2}$ *[1 mark]*
   *[3 marks available in total — as above]*

## Page 35: Quadratic Equations

1  3 and 6 multiply to give 18 and add to give 9,
   so $x^2 + 9x + 18 = (x + 3)(x + 6)$
   *[2 marks available — 1 mark for the correct numbers in the brackets, 1 mark for the correct signs]*
   The brackets can be either way around — $(x + 6)(x + 3)$ is also correct.

2  1 and 5 multiply to give 5 and subtract to give –4,
   so $y^2 - 4y - 5 = (y + 1)(y - 5)$
   *[2 marks available — 1 mark for the correct numbers in the brackets, 1 mark for the correct signs]*

3  4 and 8 multiply to give 32 and subtract to give 4,
   so $x^2 + 4x - 32 = (x - 4)(x + 8)$
   *[2 marks available — 1 mark for the correct numbers in the brackets, 1 mark for the correct signs]*

4  a)  4 and 5 multiply to give 20 and add to give 9,
       so $x^2 - 9x + 20 = (x - 4)(x - 5)$
       *[2 marks available — 1 mark for the correct numbers in the brackets, 1 mark for the correct signs]*
    b)  $x - 4 = 0$ or $x - 5 = 0$
       $x = 4$      $x = 5$
       *[1 mark for both solutions correct]*

Answers

5 6 and 2 multiply to give 12 and subtract to give 4,
  so $x^2 + 4x - 12 = (x + 6)(x - 2)$
  *[1 mark for the correct numbers in the brackets,
  1 mark for the correct signs]*
  $x + 6 = 0$ or $x - 2 = 0$
  $x = -6$    $x = 2$
  *[1 mark for both solutions]*
  *[3 marks available in total — as above]*

### Page 36: Trial and Improvement

1 E.g.

| $x$ | $x^3 + 4x$ | Notes |
|---|---|---|
| 2 | 16 | too small |
| 3 | 39 | too big |
| 2.5 | 25.625 | too big |
| 2.3 | 21.367 | too small |
| 2.4 | 23.424 | too small |
| 2.45 | 24.506... | too big |

$x = 2.4$
*[4 marks available — 1 mark for any trial between 2 and 3, 1 mark for any trial between 2 and 2.5, 1 mark for an appropriate trial to 2 d.p., 1 mark for the correct answer]*

2 E.g.

| $x$ | $x^3 + 5x - 12$ | Notes |
|---|---|---|
| 1 | -6 | too small |
| 2 | 6 | too big |
| 1.5 | -1.125 | too small |
| 1.7 | 1.413 | too big |
| 1.6 | 0.096 | too big |
| 1.55 | -0.526... | too small |

$x = 1.6$
*[4 marks available — 1 mark for any trial between 1 and 2, 1 mark for any trial between 1.5 and 2, 1 mark for an appropriate trial to 2 d.p., 1 mark for the correct answer]*

3 E.g.

| $x$ | $x^2(x + 1)$ | Notes |
|---|---|---|
| 3 | 36 | too small |
| 4 | 80 | too big |
| 3.5 | 55.125 | too small |
| 3.7 | 64.343 | too big |
| 3.6 | 59.616 | too small |
| 3.65 | 61.949... | too small |

$x = 3.7$
*[4 marks available — 1 mark for any trial between 3 and 4, 1 mark for any trial between 3.5 and 4, 1 mark for an appropriate trial to 2 d.p., 1 mark for the correct answer]*

### Pages 37-38: Sequences

1 The first term in this sequence is $(3 \times 1) + 2 = 5$
  The second term in this sequence is $(3 \times 2) + 2 = 8$
  The third term in this sequence is $(3 \times 3) + 2 = 11$
  So the first 3 terms in this sequence are 5, 8 and 11.
  *[2 marks available — 2 marks for all three correct terms, otherwise 1 mark for any two correct terms]*

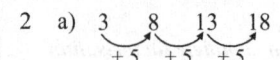

2 a) 3  8  13  18
       +5 +5 +5
  The common difference is 5, so the next two terms in the sequence will be $18 + 5 = 23$ and $23 + 5 = 28$. *[1 mark]*

  b) The common difference is 5 so $5n$ is in the formula.
  $5n$:  5  10  15  20
         ↓-2 ↓-2 ↓-2 ↓-2
  term:  3   8  13  18
  You have to subtract 2 to get to the term, so the expression for the $n$th term is $5n - 2$.
  *[2 marks available — 2 marks for correct expression, otherwise 1 mark for finding 5n]*
  You could also have found the nth term using the equation nth term = dn + (a − d), where d is the common difference (in this case 5) and a is the first term (in this case 3).

  c) $5 \times 30 - 2 = 150 - 2 = 148$ *[1 mark]*

3 a) The differences between the terms are 2, 4, 6, 8, ... so to find the next term, add 10 onto 24: $24 + 10 = 34$.
  Then add 12 onto 34: $34 + 12 = 46$.
  *[2 marks available — 1 mark for each correct term]*

  b) $100^2 - 100 + 10 = 10000 - 100 + 10 = 9910$ *[1 mark]*

4 a) Number of grey squares as a sequence: 1, 5, 9, 13, ...
  Common difference = 4 so $4n$ is in the formula.
  To get from $4n$ to each term, you have to subtract 3, so the expression for the $n$th term is $4n - 3$.
  *[2 marks available — 2 marks for correct expression, otherwise 1 mark for finding 4n]*

  b) Total number of squares as a sequence: 1, 7, 17, 31, ...
  First difference: 6, 10, 14
  Second difference: 4, 4
  So the difference between the number of squares in consecutive patterns increases by 4 each time.
  Total number of squares in the...
  ...fifth pattern = $31 + (14 + 4) = 31 + 18 = 49$
  ...sixth pattern = $49 + (18 + 4) = 49 + 22 = 71$
  ...seventh pattern = $71 + (22 + 4) = 71 + 26 = 97$
  So the first pattern to contain more than 75 squares will be the seventh.
  *[3 marks available — 1 mark for finding that the second difference is 4, 1 mark for correctly finding the number of squares in the sixth or seventh pattern, 1 mark for the correct answer]*
  You could also answer this question by looking at the pictures of the patterns. You'll still get all the marks if you get the correct answer and show your working.

5 a) The differences between the terms are 4, 6, 8, ... so to find the next term, add 10 onto 20: $20 + 10 = 30$.
  Then add 12 onto 30: $30 + 12 = 42$.
  *[2 marks available — 1 mark for each correct term]*

  b) Sequence:       2    6   12   20
     First difference:  4    6    8
     Second difference:  2    2  *[1 mark]*
  Coefficient of $n^2 = 2 \div 2 = 1$
  Actual sequence − $n^2$ sequence:
              1   2   3   4
  Difference:   1   1   1
  So this is a linear sequence with $n$th term $n$ *[1 mark]*.
  So the $n$th term is $n^2 + n$ *[1 mark]*.
  *[3 marks available in total — as above]*

## Pages 39-40: Inequalities

1. $-3, -2, -1, 0, 1$
   *[2 marks available — 2 marks for all five numbers correct, otherwise 1 mark for four correct numbers]*

2. $9 < 2p \leq 18$, so $4.5 < p \leq 9$ *[1 mark]*
   $p = 5, 6, 7, 8, 9$ *[2 marks for all five numbers correct, otherwise 1 mark for four correct numbers]*
   *[3 marks available in total — as above]*

3. a) $6q - 8 < 40$, so $6q < 48$ *[1 mark]* and $q < 8$ *[1 mark]*
   *[2 marks available in total — as above]*
   b) $\frac{3x}{4} \leq 9$, so $3x \leq 36$ *[1 mark]* and $x \leq 12$ *[1 mark]*
   *[2 marks available in total — as above]*

4. a) $7x - 2 < 2x - 42$, so $5x < -40$ *[1 mark]* and $x < -8$ *[1 mark]*
   *[2 marks available in total — as above]*
   b) $9 - 4x > 17 - 2x$, so $-8 > 2x$ *[1 mark]* and $x < -4$ *[1 mark]*
   *[2 marks available in total — as above]*

5. $3 \leq 2p + 5 \leq 15$, so $-2 \leq 2p \leq 10$ *[1 mark]*, so $-1 \leq p \leq 5$ *[1 mark]*
   *[2 marks available in total — as above]*

6. $5n - 3 \leq 17$, so $5n \leq 20$, so $n \leq 4$
   $2n + 6 > 8$, so $2n > 2$, so $n > 1$
   Putting these together gives $1 < n \leq 4$, so $n = 2, 3, 4$
   *[4 marks available — 1 mark for a correct method to solve at least one of the inequalities, 1 mark for $n \leq 4$, 1 mark for $n > 1$, 1 mark for the correct final answer]*

7. Volume of cuboid A = $4 \times 3 \times 5 = 60$ cm³ *[1 mark]*
   Volume of cuboid B = $3 \times 6 \times (x - 1) = 18(x - 1)$ cm³ *[1 mark]*
   $60 < 18(x - 1)$
   $60 < 18x - 18$ *[1 mark]*
   $78 < 18x$, so $x > 78 \div 18 = 4.33...$ *[1 mark]*
   Least value of $x = 5$ *[1 mark]*
   *[2 marks for OCW — 1 mark for presenting the answer in a structured, clear and logical way, 1 mark for showing all the working with few errors in spelling, punctuation and grammar and using appropriate terminology]*
   *[7 marks available in total — as above]*

## Page 41: Simultaneous Equations

1. $x + 3y = 11 \xrightarrow{\times 3} 3x + 9y = 33$

   $\begin{array}{l} 3x + 9y = 33 \\ \underline{3x + \ y = 9 \ -} \\ \ \ \ \ \ 8y = 24 \\ \ \ \ \ \ \ \ y = 3 \end{array}$  $\begin{array}{l} x + 3y = 11 \\ x + (3 \times 3) = 11 \\ x = 11 - 9 \\ x = 2 \end{array}$

   *[4 marks available in total — 1 mark for a reasonable attempt to eliminate one variable, 1 mark for the correct first variable, 1 mark for a correct substitution to find the second variable, 1 mark for the correct second variable]*
   For all the simultaneous equation questions, you could have eliminated the other variable and/or substituted into the other equation — you'd get the marks either way.

2. $l = 2c$ and $c = l - 4$ *[1 mark for both]*
   $\Rightarrow c = 2c - 4 \Rightarrow 0 = c - 4 \Rightarrow c = 4$ *[1 mark]*
   When $c = 4$, $l = 2 \times 4 = 8$, i.e. the distance from the mast to Llandudno is 8 km and to Colwyn Bay is 4 km *[1 mark for both]*.
   *[3 marks available in total — as above]*

3. $2x + 3y = 12 \xrightarrow{\times 5} 10x + 15y = 60$
   $5x + 4y = 9 \xrightarrow{\times 2} 10x + 8y = 18$

   $\begin{array}{l} 10x + 15y = 60 \\ \underline{10x + \ 8y = 18 \ -} \\ \ \ \ \ \ \ \ 7y = 42 \\ \ \ \ \ \ \ \ \ \ y = 6 \end{array}$  $\begin{array}{l} 2x + 3y = 12 \\ 2x = 12 - (3 \times 6) \\ 2x = -6 \\ x = -3 \end{array}$

   *[4 marks available in total — 1 mark for a reasonable attempt to eliminate one variable, 1 mark for the correct first variable, 1 mark for a correct substitution to find the second variable, 1 mark for the correct second variable]*

4. $95° + 90° + x° + 2y° = 360° \Rightarrow x + 2y = 175$
   (angles in a quadrilateral add up to 360°)
   $25° + x° + y° = 180° \Rightarrow x + y = 155$
   (angles in a triangle add up to 180°)

   $\begin{array}{l} x + 2y = 175 \\ \underline{x + \ y = 155 \ -} \\ \ \ \ \ \ y = 20 \end{array}$  $\begin{array}{l} x + y = 155 \\ x = 155 - 20 \\ x = 135 \end{array}$

   *[6 marks available in total — 1 mark for the correct equation from the angles in a quadrilateral, 1 mark for the correct equation from the angles in a triangle, 1 mark for a reasonable attempt to eliminate one variable, 1 mark for the correct first variable, 1 mark for a correct substitution to find the second variable, 1 mark for the correct second variable]*

## Pages 42-43: Solving Equations Using Graphs

1. $x = 3$ and $y = 4$ *[1 mark]*
   These are the x- and y-coordinates of the point where the two lines cross.

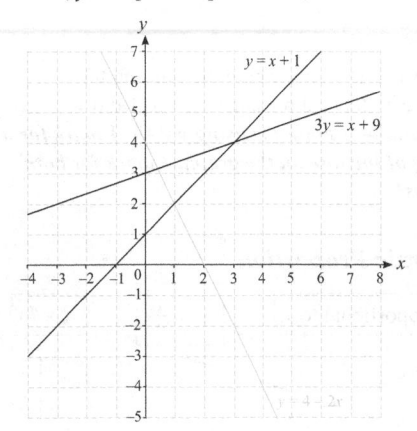

2. a) $x = 1, y = 2$ *[1 mark]*
   b)
   
   $x = 3, y = 4$
   *[2 marks available — 1 mark for correctly drawing the line $3y = x + 9$, 1 mark for the correct answer]*

3. a) Point $P$ is the point where $y = 18 - 3x$ crosses the x-axis, so $y = 0$.
   $0 = 18 - 3x$, so $3x = 18 \Rightarrow x = 6$
   So, the coordinates of point $P$ are $(6, 0)$. *[1 mark]*
   b) Point $Q$ is the point where the two lines intersect, so solve the simultaneous equations $y = 18 - 3x$ and $y = 2x - 2$:
   $3x + y = 18$ and $2x - y = 2$
   Adding the equations gives: $5x = 20$, so $x = 4$.
   Substituting this value into $y = 2x - 2$ gives $y = 6$.
   So, the coordinates of point $Q$ are $(4, 6)$.
   *[4 marks available in total — 1 mark for a reasonable attempt to eliminate one variable, 1 mark for the correct first coordinate, 1 mark for a correct substitution to find the second coordinate, 1 mark for the correct second coordinate]*
   You could have done this one by setting the two equations equal to each other and solving for x, then using your x-value to find y.

4. a) $x = 1$ and $x = 2$ *[1 mark]*
   b) Using the line $y = 6$, the graphs intersect at $(-1, 6)$ and $(4, 6)$. So, the solutions are $x = -1$ and $x = 4$.
   *[2 marks available — 1 mark for using the line $y = 6$, 1 mark for both correct solutions]*

5  Find the equation of the line that should be drawn:
$x^2 - x = 3$
$x^2 - x - 4 = 3 - 4$
$x^2 - x - 4 = -1$
So draw the line $y = -1$ to find the solutions.

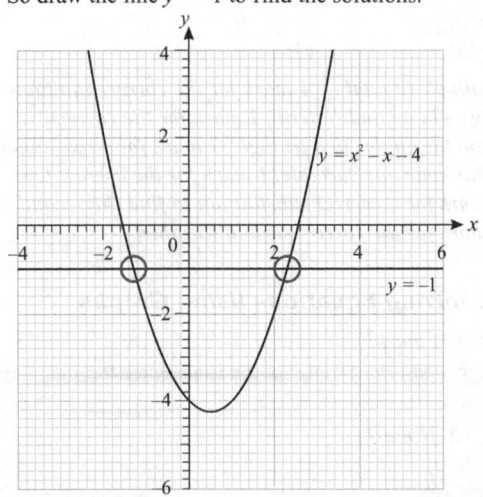

The solutions to $x^2 - x = 3$ are where the line and the curve intersect: $x = 2.3$ (1 d.p.) and $x = -1.3$ (1 d.p.)
*[3 marks available — 1 mark for using $y = -1$, 1 mark for a correct drawing of the line on the graph, 1 mark for both correct solutions]*

## Page 44: Algebraic Proportion

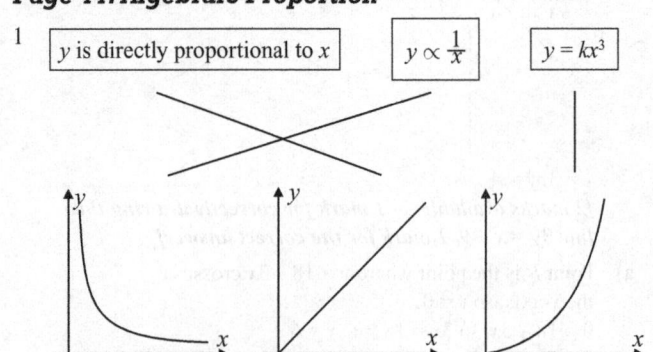

1  *y* is directly proportional to *x* — middle graph (straight line through origin)
$y \propto \frac{1}{x}$ — left graph (reciprocal curve)
$y = kx^3$ — right graph (cubic curve)
*[2 marks available — 2 marks for all three correct, otherwise 1 mark for one correct]*

2  
| true | false |
|------|-------|
| **true** | false |
| true | **false** |
| **true** | false |
| true | **false** |

*[2 marks available – 2 marks for all four correct, otherwise 1 mark for any three correct]*

## Page 45: Coordinates and Midpoints

1  a)  $\left(\frac{6+(-4)}{2}, \frac{2+1}{2}\right)$ *[1 mark]* = (1, 1.5) *[1 mark]*
*[2 marks available in total — as above]*

b)  $\frac{(6+a)}{2} = 3$ so $a = 6 - 6 = 0$
$\frac{2+b}{2} = 5$ so $b = 10 - 2 = 8$
*[2 marks available — 1 mark for each correct a and b value]*

2  a)  **L** meets the *x*-axis when $y = 0$, so $0 = 2x - 3 \Rightarrow x = 1.5$
So the coordinates are (1.5, 0). *[1 mark]*

b)  (3, 3) *[1 mark]*

c)  $\left(\frac{5+0}{2}, \frac{7+(-3)}{2}\right)$ *[1 mark]* = (2.5, 2) *[1 mark]*
*[2 marks available in total — as above]*

## Pages 46-47: Straight Lines

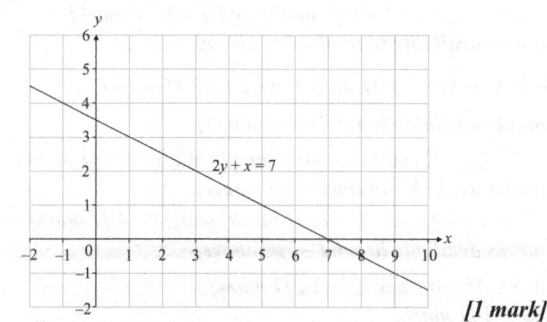

1  *[1 mark]*
To draw straight line graphs, you could either create a table of values and plot the points, or you could set $y = 0$ and $x = 0$ and join up the points.

2  a)  $\frac{(3-1)}{(-1-0)} = -2$ *[1 mark]*

b)  Gradient of line b = $\frac{(1-0)}{(1-0)} = 1$
So the parallel line is $y = x + 2$ *[1 mark]*

c)  Gradient of line c = $\frac{(-2--3)}{(2-0)} = \frac{1}{2}$ *[1 mark]*
So the perpendicular line will have gradient $-1 \div \frac{1}{2} = -2$
which is equation $y = -2x + 2$ *[1 mark]*
*[2 marks available in total — as above]*

3  a)  $m = \frac{-7-17}{5-(-1)} = -4$ *[1 mark]*
Using $y = mx + c$ and the point (5, −7):
$-7 = -4 \times 5 + c = -20 + c$ so $c = -7 + 20 = 13$
So $y = -4x + 13$
*[2 marks for the correct equation, otherwise 1 mark for $y = -4x + k$ or $y = kx + 13$ with an incorrect k]*
*[3 marks available in total — as above]*

b)  Since the lines are parallel, $m = -4$. *[1 mark]*
Using $y = mx + c$ and the point (1, −3):
$-3 = -4 \times 1 + c = -4 + c$ so $c = -3 + 4 = 1$
So $y = -4x + 1$ *[1 mark]*
*[2 marks available in total — as above]*

4  a)  Rearrange $3x + 4y = 12$ to give $y = 3 - \frac{3}{4}x$
Find the gradient (*m*) by comparing to $y = mx + c$:
$m = -\frac{3}{4}$ *[1 mark]*

b)  When $y = 0$, $x = 4$ so *Q* is (4, 0) *[1 mark]*

c)  At $x = 0$, $4y = 12$, so $y = 3$. So *P* is the point (0, 3) *[1 mark]* which means the *y*-intercept of Line **B** is 3.
The gradient of Line **B** is $\frac{(3-0)}{(0-(-1))} = 3$
So, the equation of line **B** is $y = 3x + 3$
*[2 marks for the correct equation, otherwise 1 mark for $y = 3x + k$ or $y = kx + 3$ with an incorrect k]*
*[3 marks available in total — as above]*

## Pages 48-49: Quadratic Graphs

1  a)

| x | −4 | −3 | −2 | −1 | 0 | 1 | 2 |
|---|---|---|---|---|---|---|---|
| y | 3 | −2 | −5 | −6 | −5 | −2 | 3 |

*[2 marks available — 2 marks for all answers correct, otherwise 1 mark for at least one correct answer]*

b) 

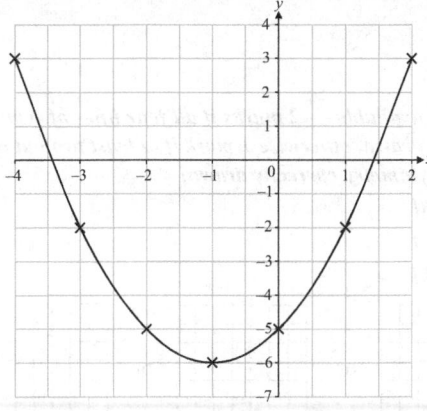

*[2 marks available — 1 mark for plotting at least six points correctly, 1 mark for a smooth curve through these points]*

c) $x \approx -3.2$ and $x \approx 1.2$

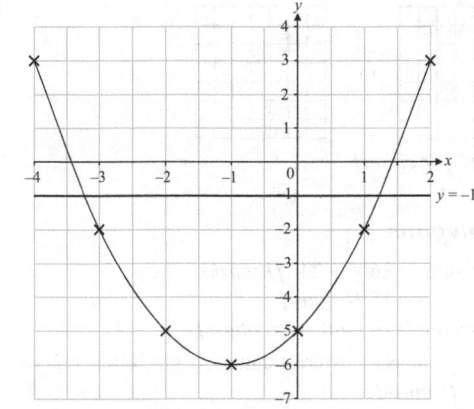

*[2 marks available — 1 mark for drawing the line $y = -1$, 1 mark for estimating both a solution between −3 and −3.4 and a solution between 1 and 1.4]*

2  a)

| x | 0 | 1 | 2 | 3 | 4 | 5 | 6 | 7 | 8 |
|---|---|---|---|---|---|---|---|---|---|
| y | 0 | 28 | 48 | 60 | 64 | 60 | 48 | 28 | 0 |

*[2 marks available — 1 mark for each correct value]*

b) *[2 marks available — 1 mark for plotting at least six points correctly, 1 mark for a smooth curve through these points]*

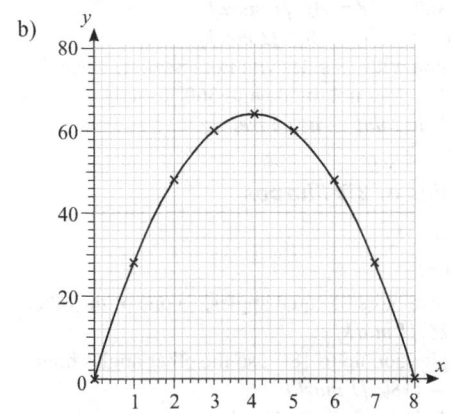

c) (4, 64) *[1 mark]*

3  The lowest point of $y = 2x^2$ will be at the origin (0, 0), so the lowest point of $y = 2x^2 - 8$ will be at (0, −8).
The x-intercepts will be where $0 = 2x^2 - 8$
$\Rightarrow 2x^2 = 8 \Rightarrow x^2 = 4 \Rightarrow x = \pm 2$

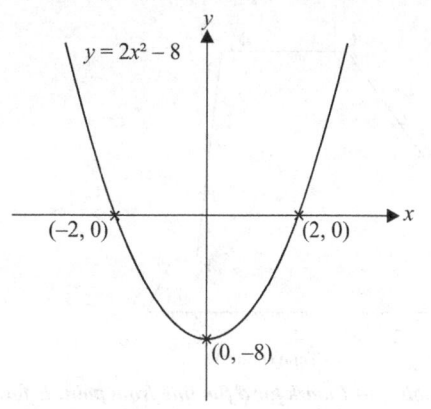

*[3 marks available — 1 mark for a convex curve, symmetric about the y-axis, 1 mark for the correct lowest point, 1 mark for both correct x-intercepts]*

## Page 50: Real-Life Graphs

1  a) 

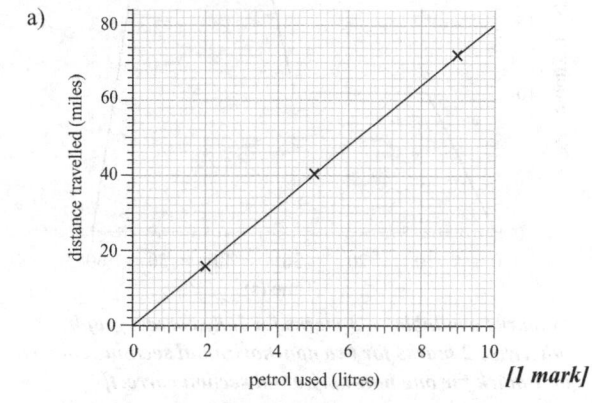

*[1 mark]*

b) Gradient = $\dfrac{\text{change in } y}{\text{change in } x} = \dfrac{80 - 0}{10 - 0} = 8$ *[1 mark]*

c) Distance travelled in miles per litre of petrol used *[1 mark]*

2  a) Plan A: £25 *[1 mark]*
Plan B: £28 *[1 mark]*
*[2 marks available in total — as above]*

b) Mr Lloyd should use Plan A because it is cheaper.
Using 85 units with Plan A would cost £26.50.
85 units with Plan B would cost £34.
*[2 marks available — 1 mark for correctly stating which plan, 1 mark for giving a reason]*

## Pages 51-52: Travel Graphs

1  a) 1 hour *[1 mark]*

b) Winifred. She reaches 30 km after 5 hours whereas Rahul reaches 30 km after 6 hours. *[1 mark]*

c) Gradient = $\dfrac{\text{change in } y}{\text{change in } x} = \dfrac{25 - 15}{3 - 1.5} = \dfrac{10}{1.5} = 6.67$ km/h (2 d.p.)

*[2 marks available — 2 marks for correct answer, otherwise 1 mark for choosing correct x and y values]*

d) E.g. Rahul is the most likely to have been injured.
The gradient of Rahul's line decreases towards the end of the race, whereas Winifred's gets much steeper. This means Rahul was moving much more slowly than Winifred towards the end of the race. *[2 marks available — 1 mark for stating Rahul is the injured runner, 1 mark for a correct explanation referring to gradients or steepness of lines]*

2  a)  Speed = gradient = 6 ÷ 1 *[1 mark]* = 6 km/h *[1 mark]*
*[2 marks available in total — as above]*

b) 2.5 hours *[1 mark]*

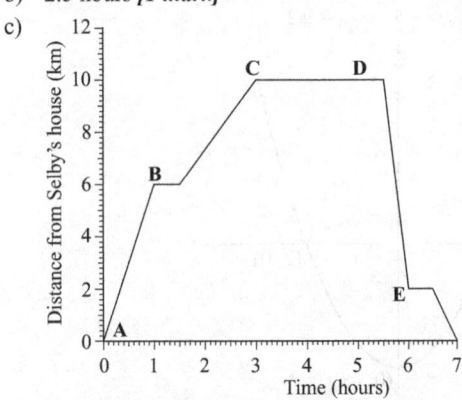

c) 
*[2 marks available — 1 mark for a flat line from point E for 30 minutes, 1 mark for a straight line from this point to (7,0)]*

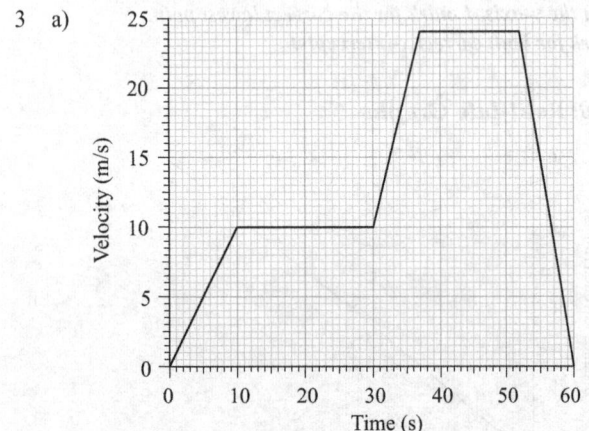

3  a)  
*[3 marks available — 3 marks for fully correct graph, otherwise 2 marks for two non-horizontal sections correct, or 1 mark for one non-horizontal section correct]*

b) At 35 seconds the graph has a gradient of $\frac{24-10}{37-30} = \frac{14}{7} = 2$.
Acceleration = 2 m/s². *[1 mark]*

## Section Three — Geometry and Measure

### Page 53: Symmetry

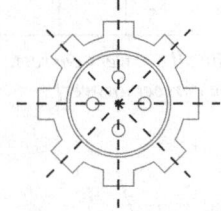

1  a) 
*[2 marks available — 2 marks if all four lines of symmetry correctly drawn, otherwise 1 mark if at least two out of four lines of symmetry correctly drawn]*

b) 4 *[1 mark]*

2  a) 2 *[1 mark]*

b) 2 *[1 mark]*

3  a)  or   or  
*[1 mark for either]*

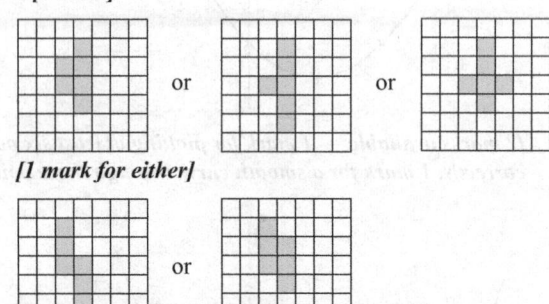

b)  or  
*[1 mark for either]*

### Page 54: Polygons

1  Number of sides = 360° ÷ 24° *[1 mark]*
= 15 *[1 mark]*
*[2 marks available in total — as above]*

2  a) $x$ is the same as an exterior angle, so $x$ = 360° ÷ 8 *[1 mark]*
$x$ = 45° *[1 mark]*
*[2 marks available in total — as above]*

b) $y$ = (180° − 45°) ÷ 2 *[1 mark]*
$y$ = 67.5° *[1 mark]*
*[2 marks available in total — as above]*

3  Exterior angle = 180° − 150° = 30° *[1 mark]*
Number of sides = 360° ÷ 30° *[1 mark]*
= 12 *[1 mark]*
*[3 marks available in total — as above]*

4  Exterior angle = 360° ÷ 18 = 20° *[1 mark]*
Interior angle = 180° − 20° = 160° *[1 mark]*
So a regular polygon with 18 sides will not tessellate since the interior angle (160°) does not divide into 360° exactly. *[1 mark]*
*[3 marks available in total — as above]*

### Page 55: Properties of 2D Shapes

1  a) 220° *[1 mark]*

b) obtuse *[1 mark]*

2  Rhombuses have two pairs of equal angles, so one of the other angles must be 62°. *[1 mark]*
Neighbouring angles add up to 180°, so the other angles both equal 180° − 62° = 118°. *[1 mark]*
*[2 marks available in total — as above]*

3  $x$ = 3 *[1 mark]*

4  a) 90° *[1 mark]*

b) No *[1 mark]*, only one pair of angles in a kite are equal, so you cannot tell if *ABC* and *ADC* are the equal angles. *[1 mark]*
*[2 marks available in total — as above]*

Answers

## Page 56: Congruence and Similarity

1. a) *[1 mark for shapes correctly labelled 'C' — as above]*
   b) *[1 mark for shapes correctly labelled 'S' — as above]*

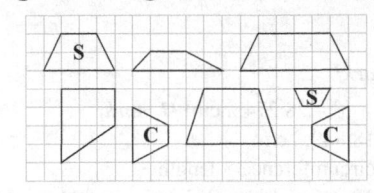

2. a) Scale factor from *EFGH* to *ABCD* = 9 ÷ 6 = 1.5 *[1 mark]*
   *EF* = 6 ÷ 1.5 = 4 cm *[1 mark]*
   *[2 marks available in total — as above]*
   b) *BC* = 4 × 1.5 = 6 cm *[1 mark]*

3. Angle *EBD* = 180° − 55° − 65° = 60°
   Angle *x* = angle *EBD* = 60° (vertically opposite angles) *[1 mark]*
   Scale factor from *ABC* to *DBE* = 5 ÷ 2 = 2.5 *[1 mark]*
   So *y* = 6 ÷ 2.5 = 2.4 cm *[1 mark]*
   *[3 marks available in total — as above]*

4. The triangles are right-angled, so by Pythagoras' theorem,
   $BC^2 = AB^2 + AC^2 = 8^2 + 6^2 = 100$. So $BC = \sqrt{100} = 10$ cm.
   If the triangles were congruent, *BC* would be the same as *EF*,
   but 10 ≠ 11, so the triangles are not congruent.
   *[3 marks available — 1 mark for attempting to use Pythagoras' theorem, 1 mark for correctly calculating the length of BC or ED, 1 mark for explaining why the triangles are not congruent]*

## Pages 57-58: The Four Transformations

1. *[1 mark]*

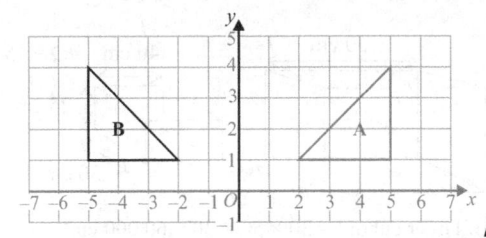

2. *[3 marks available — 1 mark for two vertices plotted correctly, 1 mark for the correct size, 1 mark for the correct position]*

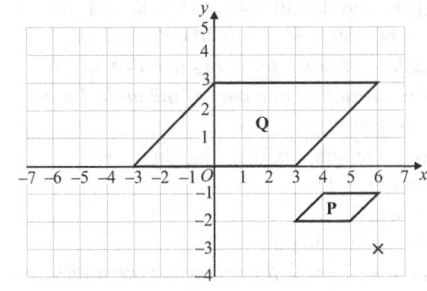

3. a) $\begin{pmatrix} 2 \\ -5 \end{pmatrix}$ *[1 mark]*
   b) *[2 marks available — 1 mark for a rotation of 90° clockwise around any point, 1 mark for correct centre of rotation]*

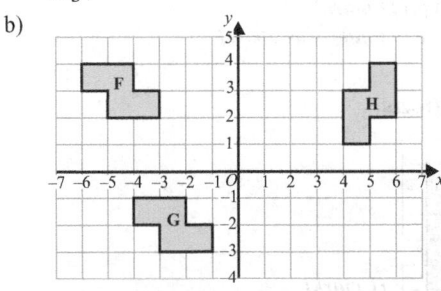

4. *[3 marks available — 1 mark for two vertices plotted correctly, 1 mark for the correct size, 1 mark for the correct position]*

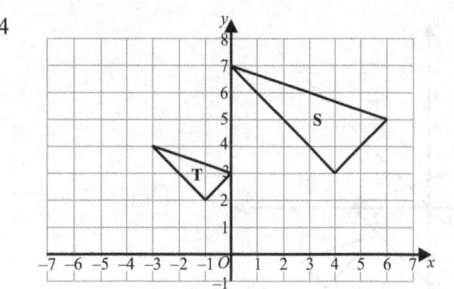

5. a) Rotation 90° anticlockwise around the point (0, 0)
   *[3 marks available — 1 mark for rotation, 1 mark for correct angle and direction of rotation, 1 mark for correct centre of rotation]*
   b) *[1 mark]*
   c) *[2 marks available — 2 marks for the correct reflection, otherwise 1 mark for reflecting the shape in a horizontal line but with the image in the wrong position]*

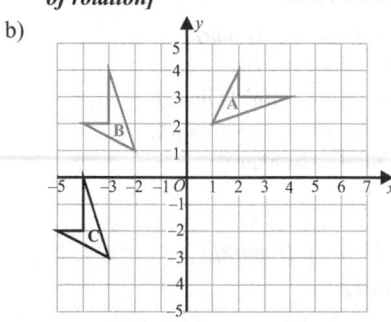

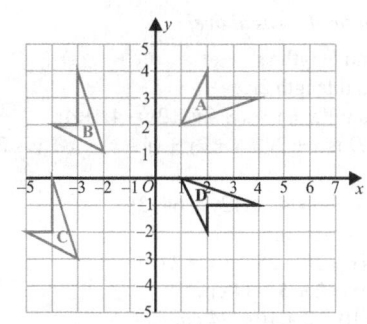

## Page 59: More Transformation Stuff

1. a) *[1 mark for the correct image]*
   b) *[2 marks available — 1 mark for a rotation of 90° clockwise around any point, 1 mark for the correct centre of rotation]*
   c) Reflection in the line *y* = −*x*
   *[2 marks available — 1 mark for reflection, 1 mark for correct line of reflection]*

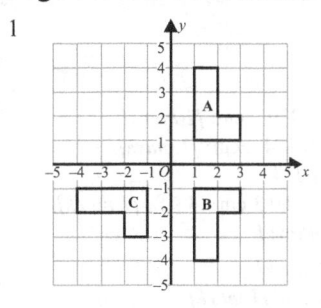

Answers

2

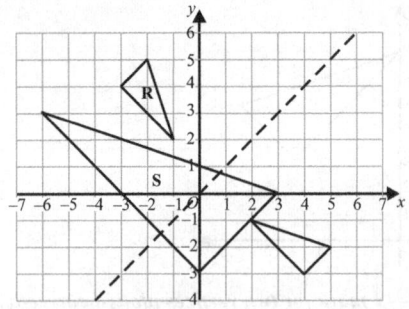

*[4 marks available — 1 mark for using the correct mirror line, 1 mark for correctly reflecting shape R, 1 mark for the correct size of shape S, 1 mark for the correct position of shape S]*

## Page 60: Perimeter and Area

1. Area of rectangle = 6 × 8 = 48 cm² *[1 mark]*
   Base of triangle = 8 cm – 5 cm = 3 cm
   Area of triangle = $\frac{1}{2}$ × 3 × 4 = 6 cm² *[1 mark]*
   Area of shaded area = 48 – 6 = 42 cm² *[1 mark]*
   *[3 marks available in total — as above]*

2. Area of a trapezium = $\frac{1}{2}(a + b) \times h$,
   so 23 700 = $\frac{1}{2}$(215 + 180) × x *[1 mark]*
   23 700 = 197.5x *[1 mark]*
   x = 120 *[1 mark]*
   *[3 marks available in total — as above]*

3. Let A have width x and length y.
   Then B has width x and length 2y.
   The perimeter of C is y + x + y + x + 2y + 2x = 4x + 4y
   and the perimeter of D is x + 2y + x + 2y + (y – x) + x + y = 2x + 6y
   So, 4x + 4y = 28 (1)
   2x + 6y = 34 (2) —×2→ 4x + 12y = 68 (3)
   (3) – (1): 8y = 40, so y = 5 cm
   Substitute into (1): 4x + 20 = 28, so x = 2 cm
   Perimeter of A = 2 + 5 + 2 + 5 = 14 cm
   Perimeter of B = 2 + 10 + 2 + 10 = 24 cm
   *[6 marks available — 1 mark for setting up simultaneous equations, 1 mark for a correct method for finding one variable, 1 mark for a correct method for finding the other variable, 1 mark for using these values to find perimeters of A and B, 1 mark for perimeter of shape A correct, 1 mark for perimeter of shape B correct]*

## Page 61: Area — Circles

1. Area of circular card = π × 5² = 78.539... cm² *[1 mark]*
   Area of cut out circle = π × 3² = 28.274... cm² *[1 mark]*
   Area of letter "O" = 78.539... – 28.274...
   = 50.265... cm² = 50.3 cm² (3 s.f.) *[1 mark]*
   *[3 marks available in total — as above]*

2. Area of square = 8 × 8 = 64 m² *[1 mark]*
   Area of circle = π × 4² = 50.2654... m² *[1 mark]*
   Shaded area = 64 – 50.2654... = 13.7345... m²
   = 13.73 m² (2 d.p.) *[1 mark]*
   *[3 marks available in total — as above]*

3. Lawn area = (30 × 10) – (π × 5²) *[1 mark]*
   = 221.460... m² *[1 mark]*
   Boxes of seed needed = 221.460... m² ÷ 10 m² = 22.14... *[1 mark]*
   So Lynn must buy 23 boxes. Total cost = 23 × £7 = £161 *[1 mark]*
   *[4 marks available in total — as above]*

## Page 62: Nets and Surface Area

1. *[1 mark]*

2. Area of cross-section = π × 3² = 28.274... cm² *[1 mark]*
   Circumference = π × 6 = 18.849... cm
   Area of curved surface = circumference × length
   = 18.849... × 11 = 207.345... cm² *[1 mark]*
   Total surface area = (2 × 28.274...) + 207.345... *[1 mark]*
   = 264 cm² (to 3 s.f.) *[1 mark]*
   *[4 marks available in total — as above]*
   The area of the curved surface is the circumference × the length because the length of the edge that meets the circle is the same length as the circle's circumference.

3. Area of one triangular face = $\frac{1}{2}$ × 4 × 3.5 = 7 cm² *[1 mark]*
   Area of one rectangular face = 4l cm² *[1 mark]*
   Total surface area = (2 × 7) + (3 × 4l) = 14 + 12l cm²
   So 14 + 12l = 98 *[1 mark]*
   ⇒ 12l = 84 ⇒ l = 7 cm *[1 mark]*
   *[4 marks available in total — as above]*

## Page 63: 3D Shapes — Volume

1. Cross-sectional area = area of trapezium
   = $\frac{1}{2}$ × (0.7 + 0.4) × 0.3 = 0.165 m² *[1 mark]*
   Volume of prism = 0.165 × 1.2 = 0.198 m³ *[1 mark]*
   *[2 marks available in total — as above]*

2. a) Split the tank into two cuboids:

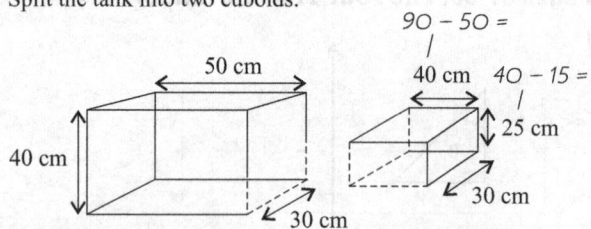

   Volume of larger cuboid = 30 × 50 × 40 = 60 000 cm³
   Volume of smaller cuboid = 30 × 40 × 25 = 30 000 cm³
   Volume of tank = 60 000 + 30 000 = 90 000 cm³
   *[2 marks available — 1 mark for using length × width × height to find the volume of one part of the tank, 1 mark for the correct final answer]*

   b) Volume of cuboid = length × width × height
   90 000 = 120 × width × 15
   90 000 = 1800 × width
   width = 90 000 ÷ 1800 = 50 cm
   *[2 marks available — 1 mark for correctly rearranging the formula to find the width, 1 mark for the correct answer]*

3. Volume of pool = π × (2 ÷ 2)² × 0.4 = 0.4π m³ *[1 mark]*
   Volume of water Amy should use = 0.4π × $\frac{3}{4}$ *[1 mark]*
   = 0.94 m³ (to 2 d.p.) *[1 mark]*
   *[3 marks available in total — as above]*

## Page 64: Projections

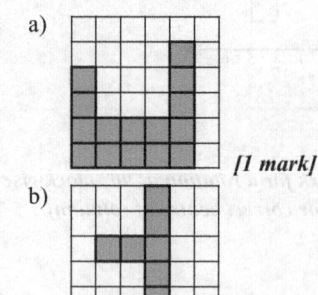

1. a) *[1 mark]*
   b) *[1 mark]*
   It doesn't matter which way round you've drawn your plan view — just as long as it's the correct shape.

2

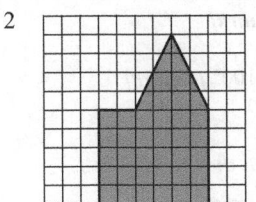

*[2 marks available — 1 mark for rectangular part correct, 1 mark for triangular part correct]*

## Pages 65-66: Conversions

1. a) If she leaves at 14:20 then she'll arrive at the bus stop at 14:50, so she misses the 14:45 bus. So she gets the next bus at 16:15. So she arrives in Rugby at 17:30.
   The time from 14:20 to 17:30 is 3 hours and 10 minutes.
   *[2 marks available in total — 1 mark for finding the time that she arrives in Rugby, 1 mark for the correct answer]*

   b) It'll take from 16:40 to 18:15:
   16:40 till 17:00 is 20 minutes.
   17:00 till 18:00 is 60 minutes.
   18:00 till 18:15 is 15 minutes.
   So the total time is: 20 + 60 + 15 = 95 minutes
   *[2 marks available in total — 1 mark for a correct method, 1 mark for the correct answer]*

2. 9.5 ft ≈ 9.5 × 30 = 285 cm *[1 mark]*
   4.6 m = 4.6 × 100 = 460 cm *[1 mark]*
   Difference = 460 − 285 = 175 cm *[1 mark]*
   *[3 marks available in total — as above]*

3. 1 m$^2$ = 100 × 100 = 10 000 cm$^2$
   So 39 200 cm$^2$ = 39 200 ÷ 10 000 *[1 mark]* = 3.92 m$^2$ *[1 mark]*
   *[2 marks available in total — as above]*

4. 150 litres × 1000 *[1 mark]* = 150 000 cm$^3$
   1 m$^3$ = 100 × 100 × 100 = 1 000 000 cm$^3$
   So 150 000 cm$^3$ = 150 000 ÷ 1 000 000 *[1 mark]*
   = 0.15 m$^3$ *[1 mark]*
   *[3 marks available in total — as above]*

5. 4.5 litres ≈ 1 gallon so 6.2 litres ≈ 6.2 ÷ 4.5 = 1.377... gallons
   8 km ≈ 5 miles so 100 km ≈ (100 ÷ 8) × 5 = 62.5 miles
   Miles per gallon for car B: 62.5 ÷ 1.377... = 45.362... mpg
   Therefore car A is more efficient to hire.
   *[3 marks available — 1 mark for converting volumes and distances to the same units, 1 mark for finding the fuel efficiency in changed units, 1 mark for the correct answer]*
   You could also convert car A's miles per gallon into kilometres per litre to compare to car B. As long as you show all of your steps, you'll get the marks if your answer is correct.

6. a) 9:55 + 2 hours = 11:55
   11:55 + 15 minutes = 12:10
   The cake is 400 g so she needs to bake it for an extra
   10 × 4 = 40 minutes
   12:10 + 40 minutes = 12:50 pm
   *[3 marks available — 1 mark for calculating that the cake must be baked for an extra 40 minutes, 1 mark for a correct method of adding times and 1 mark for the correct final answer]*

   b) 195 minutes = 3 hours 15 minutes *[1 mark]*
   3 hours 15 minutes − 2 hours 15 minutes = 1 hour
   1 hour = 60 minutes = 6 × 10 minutes
   So the cake weighs 6 × 100 = 600 g *[1 mark]*.
   600 g = 0.6 kg ≈ 2.2 × 0.6 = 1.32 lb *[1 mark]*
   *[3 marks available in total — as above]*

7. a) 3($\pi r + t$) *[1 mark]*
   b) $s^2 + 4t^2$ *[1 mark]*
   c) $2rt^2$ *[1 mark]*
   The options $s(s − r^2)$ and $t(s^2 + 1)$ are not lengths, areas or volumes. This is because they have different dimensions added/subtracted together (e.g. the first one is $s^2 − sr^2$, which is area minus volume).

## Page 67: Compound Measures

1. Population density = $\dfrac{17\,500\,000 \text{ people}}{50\,000 \text{ km}^2}$
   = 350 population per km$^2$ *[1 mark]*

2. a) Volume = 360 ÷ 1800 *[1 mark]*
   = 0.2 m$^3$ *[1 mark]*
   *[2 marks available in total — as above]*

   b) Mass = 2700 × 0.2 *[1 mark]*
   = 540 kg *[1 mark]*
   *[2 marks available in total — as above]*

3. a) E.g. 2500 m = 2.5 km. 2.5 km = 2.5 ÷ 1.6 = 1.5625 miles.
   102 s ÷ 60 = 1.7 minutes ÷ 60 = 0.02833... hours.
   Speed = 1.5625 miles ÷ 0.02833... hours
   = 55 mph (to nearest mph)
   *[3 marks available — 1 mark for converting 2500 metres to miles, 1 mark for converting 102 seconds into hours, 1 mark for the correct final answer]*
   It doesn't matter whether you do the conversion to miles per hour at the start or the end of the calculation — you could find the speed in m/s, km/s or kmh, and then change it to mph. Whichever way, you should get the same answer.

   b) E.g. time = 1.5625 miles ÷ 50 mph = 0.03125 hours
   0.03125 hours × 60 × 60 = 113 s (to nearest second)
   *[2 marks available — 1 mark for dividing the distance by the speed limit, 1 mark for the correct answer]*

## Pages 68-69: Angles and Shapes

1. 180° − 48° = 132° = Angles ACB + BAC *[1 mark]*
   (angles in a triangle add up to 180°)
   Angle ACB = 132° ÷ 2 = 66° *[1 mark]* (ABC is isosceles)
   Angle BCD = 180° − 66° = 114° *[1 mark]*
   (angles on a straight line add up to 180°)
   *[3 marks available in total — as above]*

2. a) 2x + 3x + 4x = 180
   So 9x = 180 and x = 20
   *[2 marks available — 1 mark for a correct method, 1 mark for the correct answer]*

   b) 2x + y = 180
   40 + y = 180, so y = 180 − 40 = 140
   *[2 marks available — 1 mark for a correct method, 1 mark for the correct answer]*

3. Angle CBE = 180° − 115° = 65° *[1 mark]*
   (angles on a straight line add up to 180°)
   Angle DEB = 360° − 283° = 77° *[1 mark]*
   (angles around a point add up to 360°)
   Angle x = 360° − 65° − 77° − 90° = 128° *[1 mark]*
   (angles in a quadrilateral add up to 360°)
   *[3 marks available in total — as above]*

4. a) Angle FEC = 180° − 14° = 166° *[1 mark]*
   (angles on a straight line add up to 180°)
   Angle x = 360° − 90° − 62° − 166° = 42° *[1 mark]*
   (angles in a quadrilateral add up to 360°)
   *[2 marks available in total — as above]*

   b) Angles in a triangle add up to 180° and, from triangle ABC, 180° − 90° − 42° = 48°. *[1 mark]*

5. Angle AHD = 77° *[1 mark]* (vertically opposite angles)
   Angle HDC = 180° − 122° = 58° *[1 mark]* (angles on a straight line)
   Angle DCA = 360° − 90° − 77° − 58° = 135° *[1 mark]*
   (angles in a quadrilateral)
   Angle x = 180° − 135° = 45° *[1 mark]* (angles on a straight line)
   *[4 marks available in total — as above]*

116

6  $(3a + 15)° + (2a + 14)° + (4a - 2)° = 180°$ *[1 mark]*
⇒ $9a + 27 = 180$ *[1 mark]* ⇒ $9a = 153$ ⇒ $a = 17$ *[1 mark]*
When $a = 17$, $(3a + 15)° = 66°$ and $(4a - 2)° = 66°$.
Two angles are equal and so the triangle is isosceles.
*[1 mark for substituting a into at least one expression, 1 mark for showing that two angles are 66° and hence the conclusion]*
*[5 marks available in total — as above]*

### Page 70: Parallel Lines

1  $x = 180° - 150° = 30°$ *[1 mark]*
   because interior angles add up to 180° *[1 mark]*.
   $y = x = 30°$ *[1 mark]*
   because vertically opposite angles are equal *[1 mark]*.
   *[4 marks available in total — as above]*

2  Angle $BCG$ = Angle $CGE = (5x + 10)°$ (alternate angles)
   So $4x - 28 + 5x + 10 = 180$ *[1 mark]*
   $9x = 198$ *[1 mark]*
   $x = 22$ *[1 mark]*
   *[3 marks available in total — as above]*
   There are other ways to find x. For instance,
   angles ACB and CGF are corresponding angles.
   You can then use angles on a straight line to find x.

3  Angles $EAG$ and $BDE$ are alternate angles so are equal,
   and angles on a straight line add up to 180°,
   so angle $EAG$ = angle $BDE = 180° - 119° = 61°$ *[1 mark]*
   Angles on a straight line add up to 180°,
   so angle $EGA = 180° - 156° = 24°$ *[1 mark]*
   Angles in a triangle add up to 180°,
   so angle $AEG = 180° - 61° - 24° = 95°$ *[1 mark]*
   Angles on a straight line add up to 180°,
   so angle $x = 180° - 95° = 85°$ *[1 mark]*
   *[2 marks for OCW — 1 mark for presenting the answer in a structured, clear and logical way, 1 mark for showing all the working with few errors in spelling, punctuation and grammar and using appropriate terminology]*
   *[6 marks available in total — as above]*

### Pages 71-72: Circle Geometry

1  a) Angle $BAD = 180° - 100° = 80°$ *[1 mark]* because opposite angles in a cyclic quadrilateral sum to 180° *[1 mark]*.
   *[2 marks available in total — as above]*
   b) Angle $OAF = 90°$ *[1 mark]*
   (a tangent always meets a radius at 90°)
   Angle $DAF = 90° - 80° = 10°$ *[1 mark]*
   *[2 marks available in total — as above]*

2  a) $x = 28°$ *[1 mark]*   $y = 24°$ *[1 mark]*
   *[2 marks available in total — as above]*
   b) Angles in the same segment are equal. *[1 mark]*

3  a) 5 cm *[1 mark]*
   (tangents from the same point are the same length)
   b) Angle $ACO = 90°$ *[1 mark]*
   (a tangent always meets a radius at 90°)
   Angle $AOC = 180° - 90° - 20° = 70°$ *[1 mark]*
   *[2 marks available in total — as above]*
   c) Angle $BOC = 2 × 70° = 140°$ *[1 mark]* (the two right-angled triangles are congruent, so AOB = AOC = 70°)

4  Angle $AOC = 360° - 210° = 150°$ *[1 mark]* because angles around a point add up to 360° *[1 mark]*.
   Angle $ADC = 150° ÷ 2 = 75°$ *[1 mark]* because the angle at the centre is twice the angle at the circumference *[1 mark]*.
   *[4 marks available in total — as above]*

5  Angles $ADO$ and $ABO$ are both 90° *[1 mark]*
   (a tangent always meets a radius at 90°)
   Angle $DOB = 360° - 90° - 90° - 80° = 100°$ *[1 mark]*
   (angles in a quadrilateral add up to 360°)
   Angle $DCB = 100° ÷ 2 = 50°$ *[1 mark]*
   (an angle at the centre is twice the angle at the circumference)
   *[3 marks available in total — as above]*

6  Angle $ACB = 74°$ *[1 mark]* (angles in the same segment are equal)
   Angle $ABC = 90°$ *[1 mark]* (angle in a semi-circle)
   Angle $x = 180° - 90° - 74° = 16°$ *[1 mark]*
   *[3 marks available in total — as above]*

### Pages 73-74: Loci and Construction

1  a) *[2 marks available — 1 mark for arcs drawn with a radius of 4.5 cm, 1 mark for completed triangle]*
   b) *[2 marks available — 1 mark for correct construction arcs, 1 mark for correct bisector]*

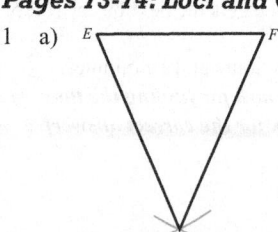

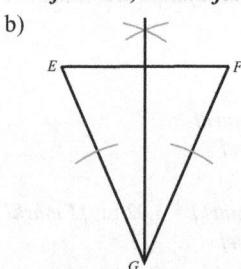

2  *[2 marks available — 1 mark for correct construction arcs, 1 mark for the correct perpendicular bisector of AB]*

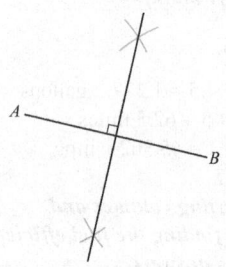

3  *[4 marks available — 1 mark for correct construction arcs for a 60° angle at S, 1 mark for a correctly drawn 60° angle at S, 1 mark for correct construction arcs for an angle bisector, 1 mark for correct bisector to create a 30° angle]*
   Here, you have to first construct a 60° angle at S (the light grey marks on the diagram), then bisect this 60° angle to give the 30° angle (the dark grey marks on the diagram).

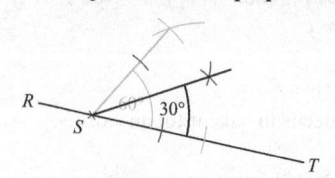

Answers

4

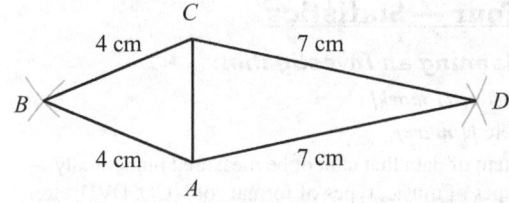

[Diagram of kite BCDA with BC = 4 cm, CD = 7 cm, BA = 4 cm, AD = 7 cm]

*[4 marks available — 1 mark for correct 4 cm construction arcs, 1 mark for correct 7 cm construction arcs, 1 mark for a correctly drawn kite, 1 mark for labelling B and D correctly]*

5

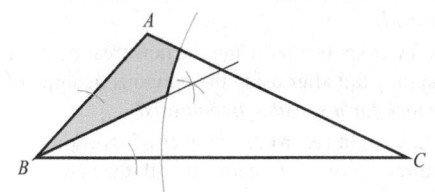

[Diagram of triangle ABC with shaded region near A]

*[4 marks available — 1 mark for radius of 6.5 cm with centre at C, 1 mark for construction arcs on AB and BC for angle bisector at ABC, 1 mark for correct angle bisector at ABC, and 1 mark for the correct shading]*

6

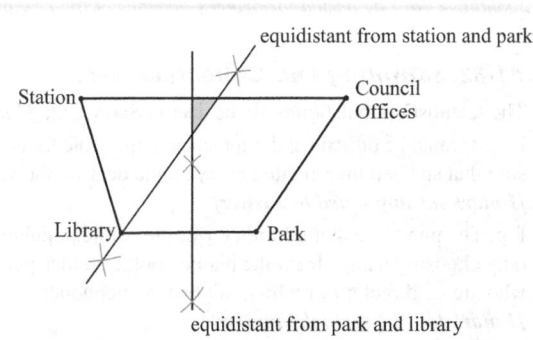

[Diagram showing Station, Council Offices, Library, Park with perpendicular bisectors labelled "equidistant from station and park" and "equidistant from park and library"]

*[4 marks available — 1 mark for the correct method to construct a perpendicular bisector, 1 mark for a perpendicular bisector between Library and Park, 1 mark for perpendicular bisector between Station and Park, 1 mark for the correct shaded area]*

### Pages 75-76: Bearings and Scale Drawings

1  a) Drawing of dining table is 4 cm long.
      So 4 cm is equivalent to 2 m.  $2 \div 4 = 0.5$
      Therefore scale is 1 cm represents 0.5 m *[1 mark]*
   b) On drawing, dining table is 3 cm from shelves.
      So real distance = $3 \times 0.5 = 1.5$ m *[1 mark]*
   c) The chair and the space around it would measure 4 cm × 5 cm on the diagram and there are no spaces that big. So no, it would not be possible.
      *[2 marks available — 1 mark for correct answer, 1 mark for reasoning referencing diagram or size of gaps available]*

2  Using the scale 1 cm = 100 m:
   400 m = 4 cm and 500 m = 5 cm

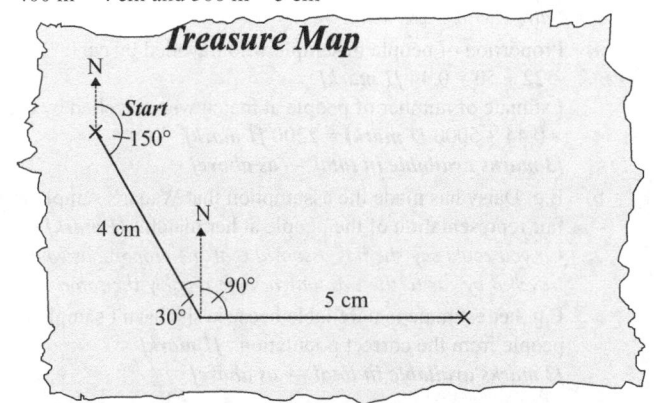

[Treasure Map diagram with Start, 150°, 4 cm, 90°, 30°, 5 cm]

*[4 marks available — 1 mark for first line on accurate bearing of 150°, 1 mark for first line with an accurate length of 4 cm, 1 mark for second line on accurate bearing of 090°, 1 mark for second line with an accurate length of 5 cm]*

3  a)

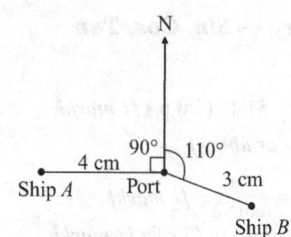

[Diagram: Ship A 4 cm from Port at 90°, Ship B 3 cm from Port at 110°]

*[4 marks available — 1 mark for Ship A 4 cm from the port, 1 mark for correct bearing for ship A, 1 mark for ship B 3 cm from the port, 1 mark for correct bearing for Ship B]*
This diagram has been drawn a bit smaller to make it fit — your measurements should match the labels given on the diagram here.

   b) 99° (accept answers between 97° and 100°) *[1 mark]*
   c) 180° − 99° = 81°
      360° − 81° = 279° (accept answers between 277° and 280°)
      *[2 marks available — 1 mark for correctly using 99° (or your answer from part b)), 1 mark for the correct answer]*
      You could also do this by adding 180° to your answer from b).

4  a)

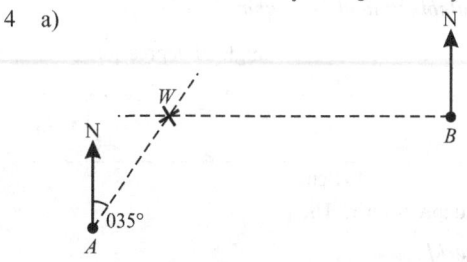

[Diagram showing W directly west of B, A with bearing 035°]

*[2 marks available — 1 mark for correct bearing of 035°, 1 mark for marking W directly west of B]*

   b)

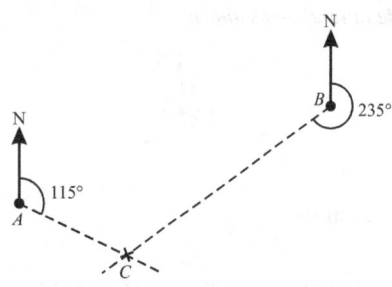

[Diagram with A at 115°, B at 235°, intersection at C]

*[3 marks available — 1 mark for correct bearing from A, 1 mark for correct bearing from B and 1 mark for correctly identifying intersection at point C]*

   c) 164° (accept answers between 162° and 166°) *[1 mark]*

### Page 77: Pythagoras' Theorem

1  $AB^2 = 4^2 + 8^2$ *[1 mark]*
   $AB = \sqrt{16 + 64} = \sqrt{80}$ *[1 mark]* = 8.94 cm (2 d.p.) *[1 mark]*
   *[3 marks available in total — as above]*

2  Difference in $x$-coordinates = $8 - 2 = 6$
   Difference in $y$-coordinates = $8 - -1 = 9$ *[1 mark for both correct]*
   So length of line segment = $\sqrt{6^2 + 9^2}$ *[1 mark]*
   = 10.8166... = 10.8 (3 s.f.) *[1 mark]*
   *[3 marks available in total — as above]*

3  Let $h$ be the height of the triangle: $13^2 = 5^2 + h^2$ *[1 mark]*
   $h = \sqrt{169 - 25} = \sqrt{144}$ *[1 mark]* = 12 cm *[1 mark]*
   The area is $A = \frac{1}{2} \times 10 \times 12 = 60$ cm² *[1 mark]*
   *[4 marks available in total — as above]*

4  Length of $EA$: $28.3^2 = 20^2 + EA^2$ *[1 mark]*
   $EA = \sqrt{800.89 - 400} = 20.02...$ *[1 mark]*
   Length of $CE$: $54.3^2 = 20^2 + CE^2$ *[1 mark]*
   $CE = \sqrt{2948.49 - 400} = 50.48...$ *[1 mark]*
   Perimeter = $28.3 + 54.3 + EA + CE = 153.1$ cm (1 d.p) *[1 mark]*
   *[5 marks available in total — as above]*

## Pages 78-79: Trigonometry — Sin, Cos, Tan

1. $\sin x = \frac{14}{18}$ *[1 mark]*
   $\Rightarrow x = \sin^{-1}\left(\frac{14}{18}\right)$ *[1 mark]* $= 51.1°$ (1 d.p.) *[1 mark]*
   *[3 marks available in total — as above]*

2. $\tan 52° = \frac{4}{y}$ *[1 mark]* $\Rightarrow y = \frac{4}{\tan 52°}$ *[1 mark]*
   $= 3.13$ m (3 s.f.) *[1 mark]*
   *[3 marks available in total — as above]*

3. a) $\sin 34° = \frac{h}{10}$ *[1 mark]*
   $\Rightarrow h = 10 \times \sin 34°$ *[1 mark]* $= 5.59$ m (2 d.p.) *[1 mark]*
   *[3 marks available in total — as above]*

   b) *Split ABC into two right-angled triangles, and find half of AC (call it x).*
   $\cos 34° = \frac{x}{10}$ *[1 mark]*
   $\Rightarrow x = 10 \times \cos 34°$ *[1 mark]* $= 8.29...$
   $AC = 8.29... \times 2 = 16.58$ m (2 d.p.) *[1 mark]*
   *[3 marks available in total — as above]*

4. Call the angle of depression $x$. Then:
   $\tan x = \frac{12}{191}$ *[1 mark]*
   $\Rightarrow x = \tan^{-1}\left(\frac{12}{191}\right)$ *[1 mark]* $= 3.595...° = 3.6°$ (1 d.p.) *[1 mark]*
   *[3 marks available in total — as above]*

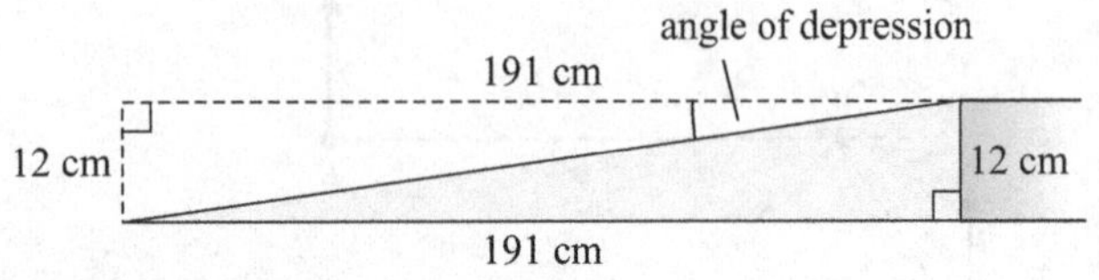

5. A three-quarter turn is 270°, so $a = 270° - 254° = 16°$ *[1 mark]*
   $\sin 16° = \frac{x}{20}$ *[1 mark]*
   $\Rightarrow x = 20 \sin 16°$ *[1 mark]* $= 5.512... = 5.5$ miles (2 s.f.) *[1 mark]*
   *[4 marks available in total — as above]*

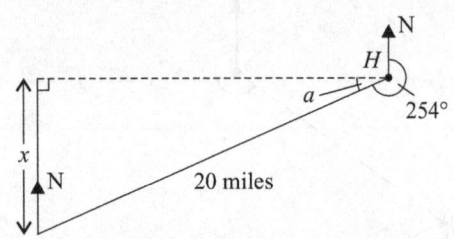

6. Find the diameter of the circle: $\tan 58° = \frac{XY}{4}$ *[1 mark]*
   $XY = 4 \tan 58° = 6.4013...$ cm *[1 mark]*
   Find length $YZ$: $\sin 35° = \frac{YZ}{6.4013...}$ *[1 mark]*
   $YZ = \sin 35° \times 6.4013... = 3.67$ cm (2 d.p.) *[1 mark]*
   *[4 marks available in total — as above]*

## Section Four — Statistics

### Page 80: Planning an Investigation

1. a) Qualitative *[1 mark]*
   b) Discrete *[1 mark]*

2. a) Any item of data that cannot be measured numerically — e.g. types of music, types of format sold (CD, DVD, etc.) or names of customers *[1 mark]*.
   b) Any item of data that can be measured numerically — e.g. takings for each day, prices of CDs or amounts spent by customers *[1 mark]*

3. a) E.g. Users had fewer spots after using the new treatment for one month than they did after using the previous treatment for one month *[1 mark for a sensible hypothesis]*.
   b) E.g. The company could record the number of spots on people's faces after a month of treatment with the new product. This would be discrete data.
   *[2 marks available — 1 mark for a sensible piece of data, 1 mark for the correct type of data]*
   *There are lots of sensible answers here — e.g. you could collect qualitative data by asking for people's opinions of the new product.*

### Pages 81-82: Sampling and Collecting Data

1. a) The scientist's population is all the deer in Snowdonia *[1 mark]*.
   b) E.g. It would be difficult and impractical/impossible for her to be sure that she had investigated every single deer in Snowdonia. *[1 mark for any sensible answer]*

2. a) E.g. The phone book might not cover the whole population — only choosing names from the phone book excludes people who are ex-directory or who don't own a telephone. *[1 mark for any sensible answer]*
   b) Increase the number of people that he samples *[1 mark]*.
   *Ten people is too small a sample to represent the whole town.*

3. Any two from:
   No time frame is given. / The response boxes do not cover all possible outcomes. / The response boxes overlap.
   *[2 marks available — 1 mark for each sensible answer]*

4. 
   | true | (false) |
   |------|---------|
   | true | (false) |
   | (true) | false |

   *[2 marks available — 2 marks for all three correct, otherwise 1 mark for any two correct]*

5. Number all the springs in the batch (from 1 to 5000) *[1 mark]*. Since $5000 \div 100 = 50$ *[1 mark]*, pick a random starting point between 1 and 50 using, e.g., a computer, calculator or random number table. Then sample every 50th item after that *[1 mark]*.
   *[3 marks available in total — as above]*
   *E.g. If the random starting point is 4, then you'd sample the 4th, 54th, 104th, ... etc. items.*

6. a) Proportion of people in sample who travelled by car
   $= 22 \div 50 = 0.44$ *[1 mark]*
   Estimate of number of people at match who travelled by car
   $= 0.44 \times 5000$ *[1 mark]* $= 2200$ *[1 mark]*
   *[3 marks available in total — as above]*
   b) E.g. Daisy has made the assumption that Waqar's sample is a fair representation of the people at her match. *[1 mark]*
   *Or you could say she has assumed that the proportions who travelled by car to the two matches are roughly the same.*
   E.g. her estimate is unreliable because she hasn't sampled people from the correct population. *[1 mark]*
   *[2 marks available in total — as above]*

## Page 83: Mean, Median, Mode and Range

1

| true | (false) |
|---|---|
| (true) | false |
| true | (false) |
| true | (false) |
| true | (false) |

*[2 marks available — 2 marks for all five correct, otherwise 1 mark for any four correct]*

2  The mean of the three numbers is 4, so they must add up to 4 × 3 = 12. Find two numbers that have a range of 6 and work out the third number by subtracting them from 12. You also need to make sure that the third number falls between the other two. 1 and 7 have a range of 7 − 1 = 6 and 12 − 1 − 7 = 4 (which is between 1 and 7), so the three numbers are 1, 4 and 7.
*[2 marks available — 1 mark for three numbers that add up to 12, 1 mark for three numbers with a range of 6]*

3  a)  Sum of numbers = 5 × 12 = 60 *[1 mark]*
Sum of known numbers = 50
So sum of missing numbers = 60 − 50 = 10
For the known numbers there are two modes, 2 and 7.
So for 7 to be the mode of all the numbers, one of the missing numbers must be 7 *[1 mark]*.
The other must be 10 − 7 = 3 *[1 mark]*.
*[3 marks available in total — as above]*

b)  The extra number 6 is higher than the mean of the twelve numbers (5), so the mean would increase *[1 mark]*

## Page 84: Averages and Spread

1  a)  (i) The time of 90 hours is much lower than the other times, and this will distort the mean far more than the median. *[1 mark for a sensible reason]*.
(ii) List the numbers in ascending order:
90, 2010, 2030, 2550, 2620, 2750, 2800, 3090
Position of median = (8 + 1) ÷ 2 = 4.5
So the median is between 2550 and 2620:
(2550 + 2620) ÷ 2 = 2585 hours
*[2 marks available — 1 mark for ordering the numbers, 1 mark for the correct answer]*

b)  The median of the second type of bulb (1975 hours) is lower than that of the first type of bulb (2825 hours), so the second type of bulb generally has a shorter lifetime than the first.
*[1 mark]*

2  a)  Patch A: 8, 8, 9, 12, 13, 14, 14, 16, 18, 19, 22
lower quartile = 3rd value = 9
upper quartile = 9th value = 18
IQR = 18 − 9 = 9
Patch B: 11, 11, 13, 13, 14, 15, 19
lower quartile = 2nd value = 11
upper quartile = 6th value = 15
IQR = 15 − 11 = 4
*[4 marks available — 2 marks for each correct interquartile range, otherwise 1 mark for each correct lower or upper quartile up to a maximum of 2 marks]*

b)  E.g. The interquartile range is larger for Patch A than for Patch B, so the numbers of strawberries per plant in Patch A are more spread out *[1 mark]*.

## Page 85: Simple Charts and Graphs

1  E.g. August lies between known points / there is no known data for August, so the line on the graph here does not necessarily indicate the number of swallows in August. *[1 mark for a sensible answer]*

2  a)  Total drinks sold on Wednesday = 25 + 60 = 85
Teas sold on Wednesday = 25
(25 ÷ 85) × 100 = 29.411...% = 29.4% (1 d.p.)
*[2 marks available — 1 mark for the correct method, 1 mark for the correct answer]*

b)  (i) Range = greatest value − smallest value
= 60 − 30 *[1 mark]*
= 30 *[1 mark]*
*[2 marks available in total — as above]*
(ii) Total number of drinks sold
= 50 + 30 + 40 + 55 + 25 + 60 + 70 + 50 + 50 + 50
= 480 *[1 mark]*
Number of days = 5
Mean = 480 ÷ 5 *[1 mark]* = 96 *[1 mark]*
*[3 marks available in total — as above]*

## Page 86: Pie Charts

1  a)  $\frac{1}{4}$ *[1 mark]*

b)  Badminton = 360 − 180 − 90 − 30 = 60°
Football = 180°, so 60 people = 180°
1 person = 180° ÷ 60 = 3°
So number of people who prefer badminton = 60° ÷ 3° = 20
*[2 marks available — 1 mark for a correct method, 1 mark for the correct final answer]*
*There are other ways to work this out — e.g. you could also use the number of people who prefer football (60) to work out the total people surveyed and then use the angle of the badminton sector to work out what fraction of the total this is $\left(\frac{1}{6}\right)$.*

2  a)  Total number of people = 12 + 18 + 9 + 21 = 60
Multiplier = 360 ÷ 60 = 6 *[1 mark]*
Plain: 12 × 6 = 72°
Salted: 18 × 6 = 108°
Sugared: 9 × 6 = 54°
Toffee: 21 × 6 = 126° *[1 mark for all four angles correct]*

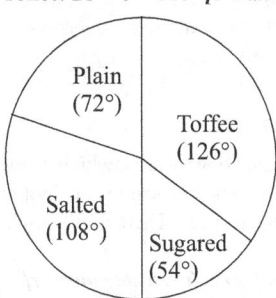

*[2 marks for a fully correct pie chart, otherwise 1 mark for at least three correct sectors but incorrectly labelled or at least two correct sectors and correctly labelled]*
*Accept angles drawn within ±2° of the actual angle.*
*[4 marks available in total — as above]*

b)  E.g. Gavin is not right because there is no information about the number of people in the ice-cream survey *[1 mark]*.
*Remember that pie charts only show proportions — not the actual number of things.*

## Page 87: Scatter Diagrams

1. a) (Strong) positive correlation *[1 mark]*
   b) E.g.

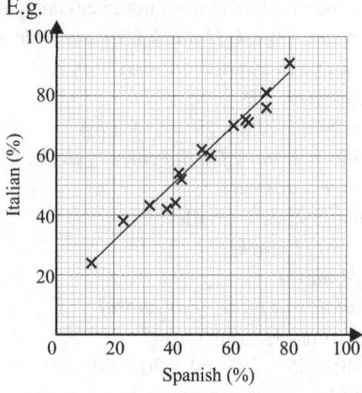

   *[1 mark for line of best fit that lies between (12, 16) and (12, 28) and also between (80, 82) and (80, 96)]*

   c) 56% *[1 mark]*.
   Accept answers between 54% and 60%.

2. a)

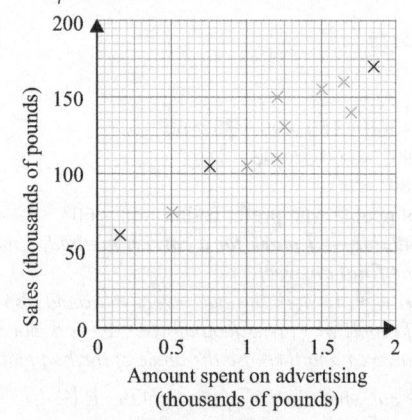

   *[1 mark if all three points are plotted correctly]*

   b) E.g. I disagree with his statement. Advertising and sales are correlated, but an increase in advertising might not actually cause an increase in sales.
   *[1 mark for stating you disagree and any sensible explanation]*
   There could be other factors that cause sales to increase — e.g. selling furniture at cheaper prices.

## Page 88: Interpreting Data

1. E.g. The horizontal axis is angled downwards, which exaggerates the increasing trend of the line. / The vertical axis is broken, which makes the rise in the line seem steeper. / There aren't any units on the horizontal axis.
   *[2 marks available — 1 mark for each sensible answer]*

2. The interquartile range *[1 mark]*, because the data value of 4 is an outlier and so would unduly affect the range *[1 mark for a sensible explanation]*.
   *[2 marks available in total — as above]*

3. Chart 2 *[1 mark]* because Sector A has been shaded to stand out more and the 3D effect/volume makes it take up more area than it should do *[1 mark]*.
   *[2 marks available in total — as above]*

## Page 89: Frequency Tables — Finding Averages

1. a) 5 − 0 = 5 *[1 mark]*
   *No one had 6 pets so you don't include 6 in the calculation.*
   b)

   | Number of pets | Frequency | No. of pets × Frequency |
   |---|---|---|
   | 0 | 8 | 0 |
   | 1 | 3 | 3 |
   | 2 | 5 | 10 |
   | 3 | 8 | 24 |
   | 4 | 4 | 16 |
   | 5 | 1 | 5 |
   | 6 | 0 | 0 |
   | **Total** | 29 | 58 |

   Mean = 58 ÷ 29 = 2
   *[4 marks available — 1 mark for multiplying the numbers by the frequencies, 1 mark for finding the correct total number of pets (58), 1 mark for dividing by the correct total number of pupils (29), 1 mark for the correct final answer]*

   c) Position of median = (29 + 1) ÷ 2 = 15 *[1 mark]*
   $11^{th}$ value = 1 and $12^{th}$ to $16^{th}$ value = 2, so median = 2 *[1 mark]*
   *[2 marks available in total — as above]*

2. a) 100 *[1 mark]*
   *The mode is the category with the greatest frequency.*
   b) Position of median = (180 + 1) ÷ 2 = 90.5 *[1 mark]*
   There are 6 + 20 + 44 = 70 bags in the first three columns and 70 + 108 = 178 bags in the first four columns. So the 90.5 position is in the fourth column. So the median number of nails per bag is 100 *[1 mark]*.
   *[2 marks available in total — as above]*

   c) (97 × 6) + (98 × 20) + (99 × 44) + (100 × 108) + (101 × 2) = 17 900
   17 900 ÷ 180 = 99.44... = 99.4 (1 d.p.)
   *[4 marks available — 1 mark for multiplying the numbers by the frequencies, 1 mark for finding the correct total number of nails (17 900), 1 mark for dividing by the correct total number of bags (180), 1 mark for the correct final answer]*

## Page 90: Grouped Frequency Tables

1. a) 3 ≤ x ≤ 5 *[1 mark]*
   b) (10 + 1) ÷ 2 = 5.5, so the median is halfway between the $5^{th}$ and $6^{th}$ values, so it lies in the group containing the $5^{th}$ and $6^{th}$ values, which is 3 ≤ x ≤ 5 *[1 mark]*
   c) E.g. The mean height can't be 12 cm, because all of the heights are less than 12 cm.
   *[1 mark for a correct explanation]*

2. a)

   | Time (t secs) | Freq | Mid-interval value | Freq × Mid-interval |
   |---|---|---|---|
   | 22 < t ≤ 26 | 4 | (22 + 26) ÷ 2 = 24 | 4 × 24 = 96 |
   | 26 < t ≤ 30 | 8 | (26 + 30) ÷ 2 = 28 | 8 × 28 = 224 |
   | 30 < t ≤ 34 | 13 | (30 + 34) ÷ 2 = 32 | 13 × 32 = 416 |
   | 34 < t ≤ 38 | 6 | (34 + 38) ÷ 2 = 36 | 6 × 36 = 216 |
   | 38 < t ≤ 42 | 1 | (38 + 42) ÷ 2 = 40 | 1 × 40 = 40 |
   | Total | 32 | — | 992 |

   Estimate of mean = 992 ÷ 32 = 31 seconds
   *[4 marks available in total — 1 mark for all mid-interval values, 1 mark for 992, 1 mark for dividing total time by total frequency, 1 mark for the correct answer]*

   b) Number who failed to qualify = 6 + 1 = 7
   7 out of 32 = 7 ÷ 32 × 100 = 21.875% *[1 mark]*
   More than 20% of the pupils failed to qualify for the next round, so Musashi's statement is incorrect *[1 mark]*
   *[2 marks available in total — as above]*

## Page 91: Frequency Polygons and Diagrams

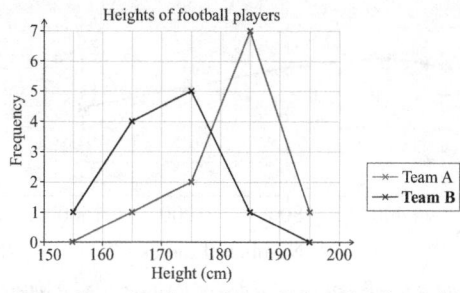

1  a) Heights of football players (frequency polygon showing Team A and Team B, Frequency vs Height (cm) from 150 to 200)

   *[2 marks available — 1 mark for all points plotted correctly, 1 mark for points joined up with straight lines]*

   b) E.g. The line for Team A's frequency polygon shows higher frequencies for taller heights and lower frequencies for shorter heights compared to the frequency polygon for Team B *[1 mark].*

2  The first bar has frequency 25, so the rest of the y-axis will be labelled 50, 75, 100. Then read off the frequencies:

| Speed ($s$ km/h) | Frequency |
|---|---|
| $30 < s \leq 35$ | 25 |
| $35 < s \leq 40$ | 100 |
| $40 < s \leq 45$ | 55 |
| $45 < s \leq 50$ | 20 |

*[2 marks available — 2 marks for all values in the table correct, otherwise 1 mark for at least one value correct]*

## Page 92: Box-and-Whisker Plots

1  a) A *[1 mark]*
   This is because the median is lowest for A (at 60 years).

   b) Greatest value = 98 (in retirement home B)
   Lowest value = 52 (in retirement home A)
   *[1 mark for both correct values]*
   Range = 98 – 52 = 46 *[1 mark]*
   *[2 marks available in total — as above]*

2  a) Median for Abbeyknock = 60% *[1 mark]*

   b) $Q_1 = 55$ and $Q_3 = 80$, so IQR = 80 – 55 *[1 mark]* = 25% *[1 mark]*
   *[2 marks available in total — as above]*

   c) The median for Blakeney is greater than that of Abbeyknock, so the students of Blakeney did better in their French exams on average. The interquartile range is smaller for Blakeney than for Abbeyknock, so the French results were more consistent at Blakeney.
   *[3 marks available — 1 mark for comparing the medians, 1 mark for comparing the (interquartile) ranges, 1 mark for a contextual interpretation]*

## Pages 93-94: Cumulative Frequency

1  a) 
| Exam mark (%) | $\leq 20$ | $\leq 30$ | $\leq 40$ | $\leq 50$ | $\leq 60$ | $\leq 70$ | $\leq 80$ | $\leq 100$ |
|---|---|---|---|---|---|---|---|---|
| Cumulative Frequency | 3 | 13 | 25 | 49 | 91 | 107 | 116 | 120 |

*[1 mark]*

   b) (Cumulative frequency graph plotted, Cumulative frequency vs Exam mark (%))

   *[2 marks available — 1 mark for plotting points correctly, 1 mark for joining them with a smooth curve or straight lines]*

   c) The median plotted at 60 gives a value of 53% *[1 mark]*
   Accept answers within ±2%

   d) The lower quartile at 30 gives a value of 43%
   The upper quartile at 90 gives a value of 60%
   Inter-quartile range = 60% – 43% = 17%
   *[2 marks available — 1 mark for the correct method, 1 mark for the correct answer]*
   Accept answers within ±4%

2  a) i) 21 *[1 mark]*
      Reading off the graph, 49 journeys took less than 47 minutes and 28 journeys took less than 27 minutes. So the number of journeys that took between 27 and 47 minutes is 49 – 28 = 21.

      ii) 4% *[1 mark]*
      48 journeys took 40 minutes or less, so 50 – 48 = 2 journeys took longer than 40 minutes. As a percentage, this is (2 ÷ 50) × 100 = 4%.

   b) The answers are estimates because they're based on grouped data, rather than the actual data values. *[1 mark]*

   c) The median of the morning times plotted at 25 gives a 26 minute journey time *[1 mark]*.
   E.g. on average it takes less time to travel in the evening than in the morning. *[1 mark]*
   *[2 marks available in total — as above]*

## Page 95: Probability Basics

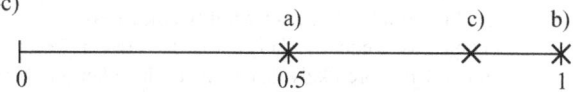

1  a)-c) (Number line from 0 to 1 with a) marked at 0.5, c) marked near 1, b) marked at 1)

   *[1 mark for the correct position of a), 1 mark for the correct position of b), 1 mark for the correct position of c)]*

2  There are four possible outcomes (A, B, C and D) and the probabilities of all possible outcomes add up to 1.
   So P(A) + P(B) + P(C) + P(D) = 1
   $\Rightarrow$ P(D) = 1 – P(A) – P(B) – P(C)
   = 1 – 0.3 – 0.2 – 0.15 = 0.35
   *[2 marks available — 1 mark for using the fact that the sum of probabilities of all possible outcomes is 1, 1 mark for the correct answer]*

3  a) P(strawberry) = $\frac{2}{2+5} = \frac{2}{7}$ *[1 mark]*

   b) P(banana) = $\frac{5}{7}$
      2 × P(strawberry) = 2 × $\frac{2}{7} = \frac{4}{7}$ so Bronwen is wrong —
      she is more than twice as likely to pick a banana sweet.
      *[2 marks available — 1 mark for finding the probability of choosing a banana sweet, 1 mark for saying Bronwen is wrong with a valid explanation]*

### Page 96: Counting Outcomes

1  a) (Hockey, Netball), (Hockey, Choir), (Hockey, Orienteering), (Orchestra, Netball), (Orchestra, Choir), (Orchestra, Orienteering), (Drama, Netball), (Drama, Choir), (Drama, Orienteering)
   *[2 marks available — 2 marks for all nine possibilities only, otherwise 1 mark for at least five possibilities with no extras]*

   b) Either hockey or choir appear in five of the nine possible combinations, so the probability is $\frac{5}{9}$.
   *[2 marks available — 1 mark for the correct numerator, 1 mark for the correct denominator]*

2  Combinations of sandwich and drink = 5 × 8 = 40
   Combinations of sandwich and snack = 5 × 4 = 20
   Combinations of sandwich, snack and drink = 5 × 4 × 8 = 160
   Total number of possible combinations = 40 + 20 + 160 = 220
   *[3 marks available — 1 mark for the correct number of combinations for one meal deal, 1 mark for the correct number of combinations for the other two meal deals, 1 mark for the correct answer]*

3  a) Total number of different ways for the spinners to land
      = 4 × 4 × 4 × 4 × 4 = $4^5$ = 1024 *[1 mark]*

   b) Number of ways of not spinning any 1's = 3 × 3 × 3 × 3 × 3
      = $3^5$ = 243 *[1 mark]*
      So P(not spinning any 1's) = $\frac{243}{1024}$ = 0.24 (2 d.p.) *[1 mark]*
      *[2 marks available in total — as above]*

### Pages 97-98: Relative Frequency

1  a) 
| Number | 1 | 2 | 3 | 4 | 5 | 6 |
|---|---|---|---|---|---|---|
| Frequency | 16 | 6 | 12 | 7 | 3 | 6 |
| Relative frequency | 0.32 | 0.12 | 0.24 | 0.14 | 0.06 | 0.12 |

   *[2 marks available — 2 marks for a fully correct table, otherwise 1 mark if at least 3 of the relative frequencies are correct.]*

   b) E.g. This would only be correct if the dice were fair and all outcomes were equally likely. From the table, it looks like rolling a 1 is more likely than some of the other numbers.
   *[2 marks available — 1 mark for saying that the dice might not be fair or that the outcomes might not be equally likely, 1 mark for using evidence from the table to explain why the dice might not be fair.]*

   c) E.g. no, each dice roll is random, so in a small number of trials like 50 she is likely to get different results.
   *[1 mark]*

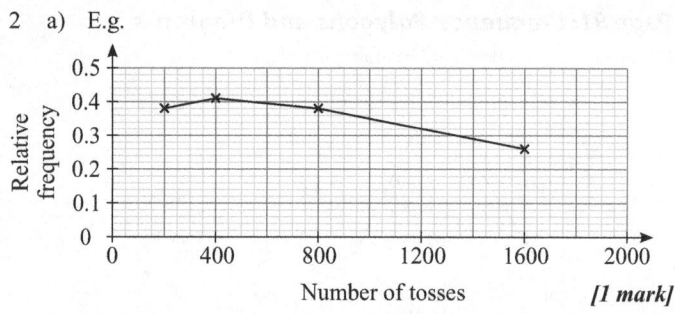

2  a) E.g.

   *Your diagram will look a bit different if you've used a different scale on the vertical axis to the one shown here.*

   b) 0.5 × 1500 *[1 mark]* = 750 *[1 mark]*
   *[2 marks available in total — as above]*

3  a) Using the graph, the relative frequency after 400 parcels were delivered is 0.03 *[1 mark]*. So there were
      0.03 × 400 = 12 parcels that were delivered late *[1 mark]*.
      *[2 marks available in total — as above]*

   b) 0.02 because it's calculated from the largest number of parcels delivered *[1 mark]*.

4  a) Divide each frequency by the total frequency (100) to get the relative frequencies.

| Number on counter | 1 | 2 | 3 | 4 | 5 |
|---|---|---|---|---|---|
| Frequency | 23 | 25 | 22 | 21 | 9 |
| Relative Frequency | 0.23 | 0.25 | 0.22 | 0.21 | 0.09 |

   *[2 marks available — 2 marks for all correct answers, otherwise 1 mark for any frequency ÷ 100]*

   b) Arlene is likely to be wrong. The bag seems to contain fewer counters numbered 5. *[1 mark]*

   c) Relative frequency of 2 = 0.25
      So the expected number is 0.25 × 180 *[1 mark]* = 45 *[1 mark]*
      *[2 marks available in total — as above]*

   d) Add up the relative frequencies for 1, 3 and 5:
      P(odd number) = 0.23 + 0.22 + 0.09 *[1 mark]*
      = 0.54 *[1 mark]*
      *[2 marks available in total — as above]*

### Page 99: The And/Or Rules

1  a) P(4 or 5) = P(4) + P(5)
      = 0.25 + 0.1 *[1 mark]*
      = 0.35 *[1 mark]*
      *[2 marks available in total — as above]*

   b) P(1 and 3) = P(1) × P(3)
      = 0.3 × 0.2 *[1 mark]*
      = 0.06 *[1 mark]*
      *[2 marks available in total — as above]*

2  a) P(no prize) = 1 – 0.3 = 0.7 *[1 mark]*

   b) P(no prize on either game) = P(no prize) × P(no prize)
      = 0.7 × 0.7 *[1 mark]*
      = 0.49 *[1 mark]*
      *[2 marks available in total — as above]*

3  P(at least 1 is late) = 1 – P(neither is late)
   P(Alisha isn't late) = 1 – 0.9 = 0.1 *[1 mark]*
   P(Anton isn't late) = 1 – 0.8 = 0.2 *[1 mark]*
   P(neither is late) = 0.1 × 0.2 = 0.02 *[1 mark]*
   P(at least 1 is late) = 1 – 0.02 = 0.98 *[1 mark]*
   *[4 marks available in total — as above]*
   *You could also solve this question by finding P(exactly 1 is late) and P(both are late) and adding them together:*
   *(0.1 × 0.8) + (0.9 × 0.2) + (0.8 × 0.9) = 0.98.*

## Page 100: Tree Diagrams

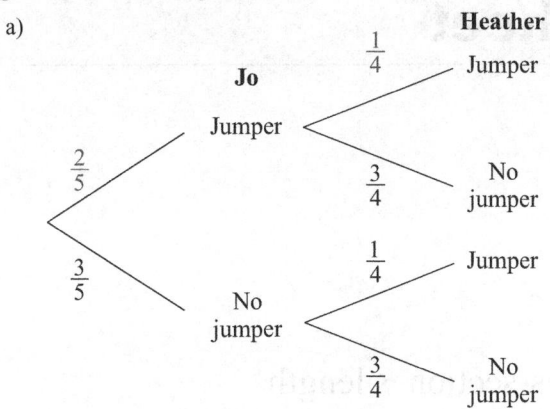

1  a)

                                **Heather**

              **Jo**       $\frac{1}{4}$  Jumper

         Jumper

  $\frac{2}{5}$              $\frac{3}{4}$  No jumper

  $\frac{3}{5}$              $\frac{1}{4}$  Jumper

         No jumper

                      $\frac{3}{4}$  No jumper

*[2 marks available — 2 marks for all probabilities correct, otherwise 1 mark for three probabilities correct]*

  b)  P(neither wear a jumper) = $\frac{3}{5} \times \frac{3}{4}$ *[1 mark]* = $\frac{9}{20}$ *[1 mark]*

*[2 marks available in total — as above]*

2  a)  P(wet and draw) = 0.15 × 0.3 *[1 mark]* = 0.045 *[1 mark]*
*[2 marks available in total — as above]*

  b)  P(win) = P(dry, win) + P(wet, win)
             = (0.85 × 0.55) + (0.15 × 0.4)
             = 0.5275

*[3 marks available — 1 mark for multiplying to find the probability of a win in one of the weather conditions, 1 mark for adding to find the probability in either condition, 1 mark for the correct answer]*

## Page 101: Probability from Venn Diagrams

1  a)  1 person didn't like any of the biscuits, so this person would go outside all the circles, so $x$ = 1 *[1 mark]*
27 people were asked in total, so
$1 + 3 + 9 + 6 + 3 + 1 + 2 + y = 27 \Rightarrow y = 2$ *[1 mark]*
*[2 marks available in total — as above]*

  b)  9 people like cookies and chocolate digestives but not ginger biscuits, so
P(just cookies and chocolate digestives) = $\frac{9}{27} = \frac{1}{3}$
*[2 marks available — 1 mark for the correct numerator, 1 mark for the correct denominator]*

2  a)  Set A = {2, 4, 6, 8, 10} and Set B = {2, 3, 5, 7}
The only number in both sets is 2, so this goes in the centre of the diagram. The other numbers in Set A go in the left part of Set A and the other numbers in Set B go in the right part of Set B. 9 isn't in either set, so it goes outside the circles.

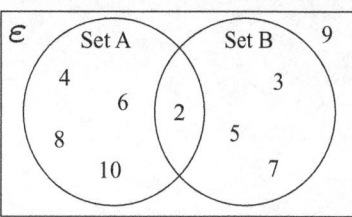

      $\varepsilon$   Set A     Set B   9
         4             3
             6  2
        8         5
          10      7

*[4 marks available — 1 mark for the centre of the diagram correct, 1 mark for the left part of Set A correct, 1 mark for the right part of Set B correct, 1 mark for the outside of the circles correct]*

  b)  There are 8 numbers that are even or prime.
There are 9 numbers in total, so P(even or prime) = $\frac{8}{9}$.
*[2 marks available — 1 mark for the correct numerator, 1 mark for the correct denominator]*

3  a)  The overlap is people who have ketchup and mustard, so this is 2%. 14% in total have ketchup, so 14% − 2% = 12% goes in the rest of that circle. 8% of people in total have mustard, so that leaves 8% − 2% = 6% in the rest of that circle.
Everyone else has neither ketchup nor mustard, so
100% − 2% − 12% − 6% = 80% goes outside the circles.
The Venn diagram looks like this:

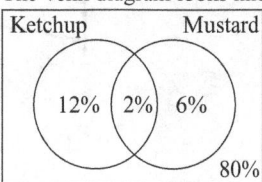

    Ketchup     Mustard
     12%  2%  6%
                      80%

*[2 marks for a fully complete Venn diagram, otherwise 1 mark for two or three correct percentages]*

  b)  There is a 12% + 2% + 6% = 20% chance that a customer had sauce. As a fraction, this is $\frac{1}{5}$ *[1 mark]*.

  c)  12% of customers had just ketchup, so the hot dog seller would expect 12% of 275 = 0.12 × 275 = 33 customers to have just ketchup.
*[2 marks available — 1 mark for correctly identifying that 12% of customers have just ketchup, 1 mark for the correct answer]*

# Formula Sheet

**Volume of prism** = area of cross-section × length

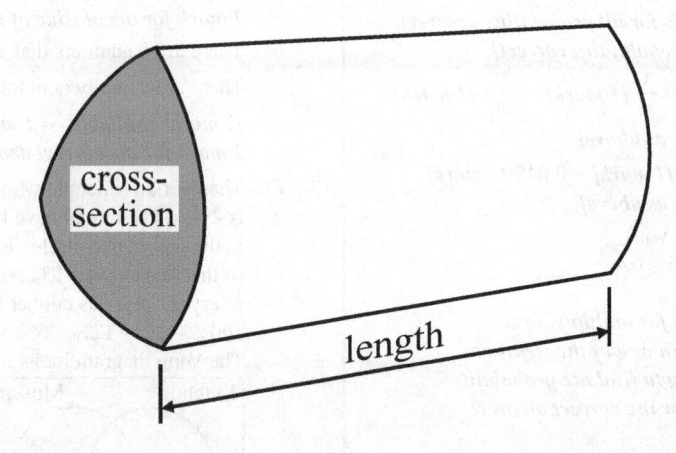

**Area of trapezium** = $\frac{1}{2}(a+b)h$

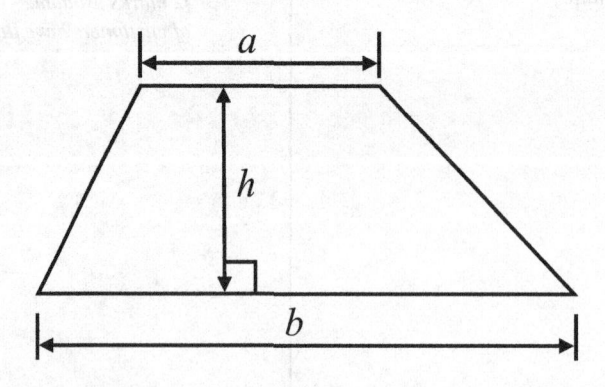